SUSTAINABLE DEVELOPMENT

Volume 13

Dam the Rivers, Damn the People

Development and resistance in Amazonian Brazil

Full list of titles in the set
SUSTAINABLE DEVELOPMENT

Volume 1: Global Environment Outlook 2000
Volume 2: Mountain World in Danger
Volume 3: Vanishing Borders
Volume 4: Atlas of Nepal in the Modern World
Volume 5: Caring for the Earth
Volume 6: Community and Sustainable Development
Volume 7: One World for One Earth
Volume 8: Strategies for National Sustainable Development
Volume 9: Strategies for Sustainability: Africa
Volume 10: Strategies for Sustainability: Asia
Volume 11: Strategies for Sustainability: Latin America
Volume 12: Wasted
Volume 13: Dam the Rivers, Damn the People
Volume 14: Rising Seas
Volume 15: Tomorrow's World
Volume 16: Social Change and Conservation
Volume 17: Threats Without Enemies
Volume 18: Progress for a Small Planet
Volume 19: Women and the Environment in the Third World
Volume 20: World at the Crossroads

Dam the Rivers, Damn the People
Development and resistence in Amazonian Brazil

Barbara J. Cummings

publishing for a sustainable future

London • New York

First published in 1990

This edition first published in 2009 by Earthscan

ISBN 978-1-84407-944-5 (Volume 13 hbk)
ISBN 978-1-84407-931-5 (Sustainable Development set)
ISBN 978-1-84407-930-8 (Earthscan Library Collection)
ISBN 978-0-41584-691-2 (Volume 13 pbk)

For a full list of publications please contact:

Earthscan

2 Park Square, Milton Park, Abingdon, Oxon OX14 4RN
Simultaneously published in the USA and Canada by Earthscan
711 Third Avenue, New York, NY 10017
Earthscan is an imprint of the Taylor & Francis Group, an informa business

First issued in paperback 2013

Earthscan publishes in association with the International Institute for
Environment and Development

A catalogue record for this book is available from the British Library

Library of Congress Cataloging-in-Publication Data has been applied for

Publisher's note
The publisher has made every effort to ensure the quality of this reprint, but
points out that some imperfections in the original copies may be apparent.

At Earthscan we strive to minimize our environmental impacts and carbon
footprint through reducing waste, recycling and offsetting our CO_2
emissions, including those created through publication of this book.

DAM THE RIVERS, DAMN THE PEOPLE

Development and Resistance in Amazonian Brazil

by Barbara J. Cummings

Earthscan Publications Ltd   London

First published in 1990 by
Earthscan Publications Ltd
3 Endsleigh Street, London WC1H 0DD

British Library Cataloguing in Publication Data
Cummings, Barbara J.
    Dam the rivers, damn the people: development and resistance
        in Amazonian Brazil
    1. South America. Amazon River Basin. Natural resources.
    Exploitation
    I. Title
    337.7′0981′1
ISBN 1-85383-067-4

Production by David Williams Associates (081-521 4130)
Typeset by Rapid Communications Ltd, Bristol BS3 1DX

Earthscan Publications Ltd is a wholly owned and editorially
independent subsidiary of the International Institute for
Environment and Development (IIED).

CONTENTS

Preface   vi
Acronyms and Abbreviations   xiii
Introduction   1

1. **Amazonian Development: An Overview**   6
   Boom–bust cycles of Amazonia   6
   Government control and "mega-projects"   9

2. **Dams in the Rainforest: What Do We Know?**   16
   Definition of tropical rainforests   17
   Tropical soils and dams   20
   Forest flooding and water cycles   22
   Species losses to reservoirs   25
   Dams and disease proliferation   29
   Hydro-development and indigenous peoples   30

3. **The 2010 Plan**   34

4. **Balbina: A Case Study**   44
   History   44
   Resistance   57

5. **Altamira–Xingu: Birth of the Resistance**   63
   The Kararão hydroelectric project   66
   Resistance   72
   Environmentalists/ecologists   73
   Social justice/minority political parties   76
   Native peoples/human rights activists   79

6. **Under the Politics of Development**   89

7. **Prospects for the Future**   102
    Alternatives   102
    Strengthening the resistance   107

    Epilogue   113
    Appendix   115
    References   118
    Index   126

In memory of Chico Mendes

Funding provided by the Hampshire College Luce Program in Food, Resources, and International Policy; The Peggy Howard Fund; Public Service/Social Change Program; The Explorer's Club; Patrick T. Knight.

Special thanks to Egydio and Dorothy Schwade; Rui and Socorro Bartolini and Paulinho Paiakan Kaiapo

Very special thanks to Marilynn and Tom

The opinions expressed within this paper are those of the author and not necessarily of the funding agencies.

PREFACE

This book began when, in October 1987, I attended a conference sponsored by the Rainforest Alliance in New York City. The conference was a meeting ground for environmental groups throughout the country to learn about the growing threat to the tropical rainforests, and to organize their forces to address the need for conservation. Representatives from deforested tropical regions such as Malaysia, India, Kenya, Peru and Brazil were present, to discuss the conditions and needs of these countries in the wake of escalating environmental destruction. The conference was an eye-opener to a student of ecology; fierce discussions about development, economics and politics went half over my head, but not so much that I missed the point entirely. At home in Massachusetts, where my previous travels in the rainforests of Panama had prompted me to join the local Rainforest Action Group, I and colleagues who had attended the conference reported on the news we had learned and launched a programme of local education and actions which would help to create support for the needs of the countries most affected by deforestation.

One event in particular was scheduled: a talk by a self-proclaimed Brazilian-Amazonian-Indian-environmentalist whom we met at the conference. Roberto Zuazo, son of an Indian mother and fisherman father, spoke at our local university and drew a crowd of over a hundred listeners. The event sparked terrific local involvement in our rainforest conservation efforts, and it was not until months later that we discovered Zuazo's intentions were quite different from our productive results.

While in Brazil, Zuazo actually spends his time denouncing conservation groups, encouraging US supporters to cut off their funding, and acting in all ways as a government agent with designs to sever the ties between Brazil and its international environmental supporters. It was a well-known Brazilian ecologist who first suspected that this was his true role. It took more direct evidence to convince me, but eventually all of the issues of development, economics and politics which had flown over my head in October hit home. Despite this revelation, while in the US, Zuazo had described to me the problems of government corruption allowing the building of disastrous dams on the Amazonian rivers. "You know the Balbina Dam in Amazonas," he confided, "it was allowed to be built because the governor's wife's name was Balbina. It is a disaster."

During the research for my thesis, I visited Balbina but never heard again about the governor's wife. And thanks to many other people, I knew the questions that would get me the information I needed, and how to ask them with great care and caution.

Being both the world's largest area of tropical rainforest and part of Latin America's most rapidly developing country, the Brazilian Amazon represents the core of the conflict between conservation and development, people and power, heritage and modernization. Preparing for a three-month field study, the question of how to resolve these conflicts in favour of the native peoples and environments of Amazonia became my focus. The research was shaped to examine the means used by the Amazonian peoples and protectors to restrain industrial development, and to strengthen the rights and values attributed to Amazonia and the Amazonians. Two primary field sites in the areas of hydroelectric developments were chosen – the region of Manaus and the hydroelectric dam of Balbina in Amazonas; and the region of Altamira and the proposed hydrolectric complex of the Xingu River in Para.

Three approaches were necessary to obtain the information relevant to this work. The first was the "simple" gathering of facts about Amazonian hydroelectric development. What were the plans? What had been accomplished? What were the effects? A large part of the research conducted in Brazil during my stay consisted of tracking down and obtaining the documents which could answer these questions. Given the nature of information distribution in Brazil, this proved to be an exercise in extreme caution and creativity. Government plans are often kept secret, particularly from certain sectors of society. Getting the answers I required meant using more the skills of a journalist than a scientist. Various government agencies supplied me with pieces of information, published and unpublished, and directed me to journals which would address my concerns. Other journalists and activists who had successfully acquired information relevant to the dams became my second source of published information. The remaining documents were picked from files which were offered to me for browsing, or opened for reference in the course of an interview.

On only one occasion was I refused information outright. This incident occurred in the offices of the government Indian agency, the National Foundation of the Indian (FUNAI), in Altamira, where a series of six dams threatens to flood the lands of 35,000 Indians. I had spent a productive and exciting two hours browsing through the files and documents kept by the agency, assisted by one of the office employees. Information on local Indian lands, government plans, and the history of regional development and opposition were in my hands and on their way to the copy machine, when the director entered. He quickly surveyed the situation and abruptly cancelled any intention of diplomatic relations with "the American reporter" he presumed I was. I was firmly informed that the plans for the dams posed no threat to the Indian people, and then dismissed. I overcame my frustration when I realized the run of luck I had had up until then. The incident reinforced the knowledge that the government keeps its sensitive plans under cover despite laws or loan conditions requiring access to and the distribution of information. The lesson was a valuable piece of information in itself.

The second means available for gathering information was the use of interviews, where they were possible. Ecologists, human rights activists and some progressive politicians were open to interviews, but many of the people with information were not, or could not be asked under the circumstances. In the text, interviews conducted and recorded on tape or in openly recorded notes are referenced as such. Other communications under less favourable conditions, or from short conversations, are regarded as personal communications. Due to a lack of published information on the dams and the inaccessibility of "hard facts", a good deal of my research depended on direct communication with the planners and the affected peoples.

The third means of obtaining information and the most significant in drawing my conclusions, was the field visits I made to development sites and affected areas. Among these were two visits to the Balbina Dam – one "official tour" and one under the guidance and more critical eye of a social-work team. A four-day stay at the forest research site of the World Wildlife Fund and the National Institute for Amazon Research (INPA), embedded the value of the forest firmly in my mind. An extended visit to the town of Altamira, where the Kararao Dam would be built, showed me a section of Amazonia in the midst of too rapid change and struggling to survive. A three-day meeting of Indian groups and scientists in Belém demonstrated the determination and organization emerging from the Indian people and their supporters in opposition to the Amazonian dams; and how far the government would go to stop them. As this meeting came to a close, the local authorities charged several participants with criminal suits for their attempts to affect development policy.

A visit to the town of Presidente Figueredo and the home of the Movement to Support the Waimiri-Atroari Resistance (MAREWA) proved to be my most pleasant and informative week in Brazil. Egydio Schwade, founder and director of

MAREWA, and the two families which comprised the organization, continuously fed me information concerning the history of the Balbina Dam and the struggles of the Waimiri-Atroari, as well as feeding me feasts of freshly hunted armadillo and the harvest of their tropical fruit trees. I stayed for a week, researching in Egydio's library and helping to chase after the children. Here, I also had the opportunity to confirm the classic Amazonian frontier town's reputation for having a "Wild West" flavour. I had spent an evening reading at one of the town's many bars, which thrive on the business from labourers who come to work on the government projects. When it grew late, and the bar became rowdy, I returned to the home where I was staying. The following morning, I woke and took a walk through the town in early light. Laid out on a table in front of an open one-room stucco house full of candles, was the victim of a fatal blow to the back of the head, suffered in a bar-room brawl which had broken out after I retired the night before. No one was particularly concerned; it was a routine Saturday night.

A visit to the Waimiri-Atroari Reserve was interrupted by sudden pressure to leave Brazil. As evidence of the sensitivity of the Brazilian government to the distribution of information about the dams, on the evening of 27 July I found myself observed by a government van and two police cars, and followed by a man suspected of being a government agent: the same Roberto Zuazo who had introduced me to the issue only a year earlier. Now, rather than encouraging me, he had me under surveillance. Without investigating the reasons for his appearance, I took refuge in a mission that night, and flew out on the morning plane. My quick departure resulted in some of my questions inevitably being left unanswered.

The majority of the information contained in this book, concerning both the dams and the resistance movement, was obtained in Brazil. Additional sources were then researched here, and hopefully fill in many of the gaps resulting from the difficulty of acquiring information in Brazil. After returning, I retained several links, monitoring events and developments in Amazonia. Through international organizations with contacts in Brazil, a Congressman's office in Washington, and the Rainforest Action Network, it was possible to stay informed of the actions and needs of the groups opposing the Brazilian government's plans for building the hydroelectric dams.

The end of this work corresponds with the end of one phase in the struggle to oppose national development plans, plans that have been imposed on the people of Amazonia and that have caused them much environmental and social impoverishment at a local level.

ACRONYMS AND ABBREVIATIONS

CCPY	Committee for the Creation of the Yanomami Park
CEDI	Ecumenical Centre for Documentation and Information
CIMI	Indian Missionary Council
CNEC	National Association of Engineering Consultants
CPI	Pro-Indian Commission
FUNAI	National Indian Foundation
IDESP	Institute for Socio-Economic Development of Para
INPA	National Institute for Amazon Research
MAREWA	Movement to Support the Waimiri-Atroari Resistance
NGO	non-governmental organization
PIN	Plan for National Integration
PSB	Brazilian Socialist Party
PT	Workers' Party
SOPREN	Society for the Preservation of Natural and Cultural Resources of Amazonia
SPI	Indian Protection Service
TRF	tropical rainforest
UNEP	United Nations Environment Programme
UNI	Union of Indigenous Nations

INTRODUCTION

The Amazon basin, located in the northern half of South America, forms one of the richest, oldest ecosystems on earth. Straddling the Equator, between the Tropic of Capricorn and the Tropic of Cancer, Amazonia is densely covered with tropical moist forest, or rainforest, the most diverse of our planet's ecological areas. The Amazon basin holds the earth's largest area of uninterrupted tropical rainforest. A full 7.8 million km² is drained by tributaries and affluents leading to the main trunk of the Amazon (Stone 1985). In its entirety, Amazonia bridges eight South American countries: Bolivia, Colombia, Ecuador, Guyana, Peru, Suriname, Venezuela and Brazil. The last of these contains the majority of the basin's forestlands and the main trunk of the Amazon River, *o rio Amazonas*. The area of Brazil's "legal" Amazonia, comprised of nine states and including the dry forests and plains bordering the rainforest, amounts to 5 million km², or 57% of Brazil's land area. The portion of tropical moist forest within these legal boundaries is termed "classic" or "geographic" Amazonia. Classic Amazonia covers an area of 3.5 million km², almost half the size of the continental United States, excluding Alaska (See Figure I.1).

The forest and riverine resources of Amazonia have long provided food, agriculture and transportation on both subsistence and commercial scales, for the native populations. Recent estimates of Brazilian Amazonia's population preceding European contact range from 6 to over 10 million. It is known that at least 230 distinct indigenous groups lived throughout the region in 1600 (Myers 1984), when permanent Portuguese occupation

Figure I.1: Brazil and Amazonia

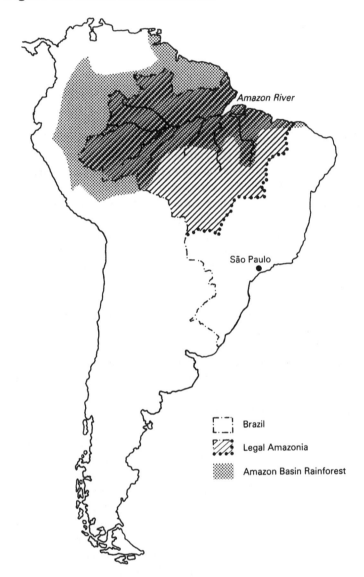

Sources: Espenshade 1986; Mahar 1989; Nyrop 1983

began. Forms of subsistence ranged from nomadic hunting and gathering to complex agricultural systems capable of providing for settlements of over a thousand people for several years at a time (Caufield 1984). Communication systems and forest corridors linked communities over vast areas, and served to transmit regional forest resources and knowledge to widely dispersed and diverse groups. With the recent exponential loss of forest habitat, the increasing scarcity of resources that the Amazonian people require in order to survive is resulting in their rapid decimation.

Since the first foreign occupations, Amazonia has been used for the economic advancement of colonial nations. (An overview of the history of colonial development will be discussed in Chapter 1.) In recent years, beginning with the founding of the new capital of Brasilia in the 1950s, an "integration" of Amazonia into the national industrial economy has overpowered the social and environmental stability of the region. The results have contributed to extensive deforestation and deculturalization in many areas. The building of roads, opening of cattle pastures, and development of the timber industry, among other projects and government initiatives, have focused international capital interests in the Amazon. As a result, deforestation from 1976 to 1978 increased 129% over *all* deforestation occurring before this time (Carvalho 1981). The most recent estimates of deforestation, based on Landsat photos, show that 12% of legal Amazonia has been cleared (Mahar 1989). The destructive nature of the occupation and development in local terms is further evidenced by the complete loss of over 80 distinct tribal groups since 1900, coinciding with the onset of North America's Industrial Revolution (Davis 1977). Among the large-scale projects beginning in the 1950s were the Amazon colonization schemes, designed to populate the interior and thus guarantee the security of Brazil's territorial claims. With promises of land ownership and government assistance, new colonists were encouraged to settle the Amazon. These people founded what are now among the poorest of Brazil's rural communities, having lost their plots due to poor soils or eviction by large landowners. They have joined the Indian people and the forest itself as victims of Brazil's plans for the economic development of Amazonia.

The depletion of natural resources and forestlands resulting from industrial extractive economies in the Amazon has not slowed, despite environmental outcry and demands for social equity by the region's people. The newest form of extraction facing Amazonia is the tapping of the energy of its rivers, to fuel the continued expansion of industry. The construction of large hydroelectric projects has already begun, the most renowned of which is the Tucuri Hydroelectric Dam in the state of Para. The purposes of the generation of Amazonian hydro-power are twofold: to fuel growing regional industries, and to supply the energy demands of the already industrialized centres of the Northeast and South of Brazil. Over half of the energy production planned for Amazonia will be transmitted to cities such as São Paulo, which have already exhausted their local potential.

Growing resistance from the peoples and supporters of the Amazonian environments are challenging the logic and the right of national plans to utilize the region's resources. While scientists and development planners know little about the workings or potentials of the rainforests, the native peoples have been living successfully within the ecological constraints of Amazonia for at least 14,000 years (Meggers 1971).

Current modes of land use and development are depleting some forest resources within a few generations. The role of the rainforests in the global environment is increasingly gaining attention. Advocates defend the value of the faunal and floral diversity of the forests and argue for benefits to be derived from the *intact* forests and river systems of the Amazon.

This book is intended as an analysis of development in and resistance to one area of Amazonian growth – the construction of large hydroelectric dams on Amazonia's rivers. In this newest phase of resource exploitation, Brazil is harnessing the energy of Amazonia to fuel the demand for export industry, in the familiar style of colonialist extraction: local resources are altered or depleted for the benefit of "foreign" nationals and multinationals. The interests of the south of Brazil and its trade nations do not serve the needs of Amazonia resulting in internal colonial-style exploitation of the region's energy resources. Three main groups of threatened and concerned peoples are identified within the movement to constrain Amazonia's industrial energy expansion: ecologists/environmentalists, social justice/minority political parties, and native peoples/human rights activists.

The focus of this research is the response to the nearly completed Balbina Dam in the state of Amazonas, and the projected Altamira–Xingu Dams Complex in Para. The concerns and methods of the resistance to these projects are discussed, with critical attention paid to the building of a movement, and to the role of the state in interaction with the participating groups.

1. AMAZONIAN DEVELOPMENT: AN OVERVIEW

An examination of the colonization and development of Amazonia reveals the long history of incompatibility between socio-economic goals and environment which has led to the continued impoverishment of the region's natural and human resources. Since its first "discovery", the land has been viewed in terms of its extractive value. Perhaps more importantly, this perception of value isolated parts of the environment from the whole. Brazil has often concentrated its activities on one or a very few resources at any given time, and is given to "mega-project" operations that are too intensive to sustain. The energy development projects of today continue to expand upon this strategy, and the consequences are indicating a continuation of Amazonia's boom–bust history.

Boom–bust cycles of Amazonia

The European discovery of Brazil is attributed to the Portuguese trader Pedro Alvares Cabral, in the year 1500 (Burns 1970). The founding of this land was an incidental boon on a voyage to India, resulting in the greatest of the Portuguese colonial claims. The chosen name of "Brazil" immediately reflected the priorities and intentions of the European founders. The country was named for its first extractive source of wealth – the brazilwood which produced a red dye highly valued on the European markets. The extractive potential of the land quickly defined the relationship between Brazil and the European colonizers, and established the criteria of value which persist to this day. In order to protect their claim against competing countries, Portugal set up permanent colonies in the South in 1532, near São Paulo, now the nation's largest city.

Permanent occupation of Amazonia, in the North, was established somewhat later. The first accounts of the Amazon were written by Carvajal, who explored the river in 1542. European settlements, in the form of forts to guard Portuguese claims, were not built until 1616. These first claims in the North were inspired by the productive sugar-cane lands extending from the river delta (Bunker 1985). Sugar was Amazonia's first boom product, and has continued periodically throughout history as one of Brazil's major economies. Extraction of native species of spice and forest goods also met with some success as export businesses.

These first Amazonian colonies and economies account for the initial major reductions in the native populations: disease and slave labour decimated the floodplain communities along the main river. As trade resources became more scarce due to years of continued extraction, the explorers moved inland and upstream and the path of disease and exploitation followed, eventually reducing the Indian populations of Amazonia to a fraction of their original numbers. With the consequent reduction in the Portuguese slave-labour force, successful extractive economies became even more difficult to sustain.

Boom–bust cycles have followed Amazonian enterprises over the years as a consequence of the overexploitation of natural resources and dependence on foreign market prices and demand. Bunker (1985) explains that in Amazonia, "colonial extraction responded to international demand by exploiting a few highly marketable resources beyond their capacity for natural regeneration, in many cases leading to environmental impoverishments, with widespread ramifications." This depletion of resources has repeatedly limited the options for future economies, often rendering the Amazon incapable of responding to world market opportunities, or to its own subsistence needs in damaged areas.

The most famous of the Amazonian "booms" is that of the rubber market at the turn of the century. Throughout the seventeenth and eighteenth centuries, Brazil's foreign trade remained dependent on a series of single major products. In 1840 Charles Goodyear vulcanized rubber, creating the pliable product that is in widespread use today, and increasing the world market demand for rubber beyond its supply capacity. Amazonia is the world centre of the rubber tree, *Hevea brasiliensis*, and exports of latex rose to record amounts. It was rubber which first transformed Amazonia from the realm of a few adventurous capitalists to a world market centre, a change accompanied by such symbols of "civilization" as the opera house built in the interior river port of Manaus. By 1853, rubber exports had increased a hundredfold. As the boom continued, the European population of Amazonia grew from 250,000 in 1853 to over 1 million in 1910 (Burns 1970). Concurrently, the indigenous population of 6–9 million at the time of contact had dropped to only 1 million by 1900 (Davis 1977).

In 1910, when the rubber boom hit its peak, 82% of the Amazonian government's income was derived from the rubber trade, and rubber latex accounted for 39% of the national export (Burns 1970). The high world market value sustained the Amazon's economy. However, in 1876 the Englishman Alexander Wickham had smuggled some rubber seeds from the country and a London enterprise transported them to plantations in Asia. As they came to maturity and were able to substitute for Brazilian rubber, the Amazonian market began to fail. The bust began in the middle of 1910. The plantation rubber was much more accessible and cheaper to produce than tapping a dwindling supply from the Amazon's rainforests. In 1915 plantation rubber had taken 68% of the world market and by 1922 it had captured the economy, providing 93% of all rubber traded (Burns 1970). Amazonia felt the weight of this bust with full force. Having been born into the world economy through rubber, it literally died after the market failed. Little was heard from the region for the next 50 years.

In the meantime, all of Brazil was industrializing and, in 1822, the country had declared independence. In order to secure the nation's new freedom, Brazil determined to strengthen its economic infrastructure. In the 1850s, 62 industrial firms were founded, 14 banks opened, and 20 steamship companies, 23 insurance companies, 4 colonization companies, 8 mining companies, 3 urban transport companies, 2 gas companies and 8 rail lines were established (Burns 1970). The Brazilian concept of security and independence became thoroughly linked to the nation's industrial development.

During the years when the Amazon was a lucrative market centre, foreign investment dominated many businesses. This has proved to be a lasting mark of Brazil's development character. In the political realm, the Nationalists of the 1900s, who believed that industrialism guaranteed security, were strongly opposed to this foreign domination of the business sector. They pushed for government control over Brazil's economic resources and were

> characterized by a resentment of foreign capital and foreign personnel, suspicion of private enterprise, a growing preference for state ownership, emphasis on industrialization, encouragement of domestic production, and a desire to create or nationalize certain key industries such as oil, steel, power, and transportation.
>
> (Burns 1970)

Finally, beginning in 1940, the Nationalists' goals began to be realized.

Government control and "mega-projects"

In 1940, foreign companies generated almost all of Brazil's electricity. The Constitution of 1934 intended to provide for reclaiming Brazil's industries, which were then held largely by multinationals. Article 119 of the Constitution read:

> The law will regulate the progressive nationalization of mines, mineral deposits, and waterfalls or other sources of energy, as well as of the industries considered as basic or essential to the economic and military defense of the country.
>
> (Bunker 1985)

In 1940, a Five Year Plan was instituted to expand and improve the nation's railways, steamships and industries, and to create hydroelectric power, seen as crucial to any plans for industrialization. The 1940s saw new emphasis being given to national mineral exploration and, by the 1950s, oil and steel industries were brought under government control (Burns 1970). Yet foreign capital continued to be attracted to Brazil's booming economies and investments in the private sector continued to increase throughout the 1950s. Foreign ownership ranged from 15 to almost 70% of some industries; the single largest investor was the United States (Burns 1970).

Government economics during this time persisted in focusing essentially on a few great resources to provide the staple exports for the country. While the economy had undeniably diversified and internalized following the rubber bust of 1910, the federal government continued to promote "mega-projects" reminiscent in scale and intensity of the previous extractive businesses which had already impoverished affected regions of Amazonia.

In 1960, Amazonia returned to play a major role in Brazil's economic development. With the depletion of resources in the rest of the country, Amazonia was seen as harbouring the last stronghold of untapped natural resources in an "empty land". Brazil also claimed concern over defending its borders, requiring occupation of the unprotected northern states. Under the Kubitschek presidency in 1960, a new capital was built in the centre of the country to link Amazonia to the industrial centres of the South, and to incorporate the northern region into the national development model.

The founding of Brasilia was a monument to Brazil's vision of the future of the Amazon. The city was designed by the architects Costa and Niemeyer in the shape of a great aeroplane and boasting the most modern of buildings and statues. The centre of the city was designed in a perfectly symmetrical division of government, commercial and touristic "quadrats", immaculate in its delivery of organization and order to the wild interior. Accompanied by the construction of the Belem–Brasilia highway cutting north into the forests of Amazonia, the lands lining the road were cleared and settled by some two million colonists to the frontier (Stone 1985).

Where previously European/Brazilian occupation had been possible only along the *varzea* floodplains bordering the rivers,

> the roads opened the terra firma to exploitation by far distant
> centres of population and enterprise. The dominant groups
> in these areas were unfamiliar with the Amazonian environ-
> ment; the technologies and organizational systems they used
> had emerged in a very different ecological and economic
> system, and they had little long term interest or stake in the
> Amazonian region.
>
> (Bunker 1985)

Plans were laid out for exploiting the Amazon's resources, primary among these being the hydroelectric energy potential of the rivers. In 1961, the administration of President Goulart nationalized commercial electricity production and created the government energy agency Eletrobras (Burns 1970). The call to develop the nation's energy potential for Brazil's increasing industrialization again looked to the rivers of the Amazon, now with the aid of a national agency to oversee the exploitation. The most complete plan for hydroelectric energy development was not presented until 1987, but during the intervening years, several projects were accomplished. The successes and consequences of these experiences have provided the opportunity for a critical assessment of hydro-power development in Amazonia.

Significant to Goulart's presidency were his populist rhetoric and programmes. The growing prospect of a peasant rebellion resulted largely from persisting foreign interests and Goulart's own encouragement of the peasant class to participate in national politics. Goulart advocated agrarian and tax reforms to a reluctant Congress and eventually challenged them by decreeing a land reform plan and an extension of the vote to illiterate and enlisted men (Burns 1970). Combined with a decrease in industrial growth and rampant inflation during his years in office, it took little time following this open challenge for the military to stage a coup. After Goulart's televised rebuke of military officers for their "lack of discipline", aired on the evening of 30 March 1964, he was overthrown and failed to rally public support. Military rule returned to the country after 18 years of democracy and succeeded in retaining power for the next 20 years, until 1985. Early in their governance, the military rulers re-established a multinational economic base by initiating incentives and protective measures to provide an attractive and secure environment for foreign capital (Bunker 1985). Throughout the following years of intensive colonization and development in Amazonia, these policies regressed in response to a level of foreign domination so extreme that it came to be seen as a threat to the national security of Brazil.

Once the military had secured control of the government again, the economic integration of the Amazon became the focus of the nation. In 1966, "Operation Amazon" was announced. Followed in 1970 by the Plan for National Integration (PIN), a far-reaching programme for roads, colonization and business interests was worked out for Amazonia. The Trans-Amazon Highway was constructed, intended primarily, according to the PIN, to give the poor landless of the Northeast access to the colonization potential of Amazonia. President Geisel announced that the extensive colonization projects were intended to provide "land without men for men without land" (Burns 1970); 100,000 families were projected for resettlement along the highway cut through the forest. The scale of this and other government projects in the industrial sector resulted in the borrowing of $3.5 billion between the coup of 1964 and June 1971 (Davis 1977). An additional $400 million was borrowed from private banks, and by 1972 Brazil had become the largest debtor nation in the world. Concurrently, foreign capital investments in Brazilian businesses surpassed previous records: up to 90% of some industries were owned by foreign subsidiaries in 1969 (Burns 1970).

The failure of the PIN to achieve its goals resulted in the revising of integration policy for Amazonia's role in national economic development. By 1975, only 7,000 settlers had been placed by the colonization programme, and infertile soils saw many of these farms failing within the first few years. But much land had been cleared and the stage was set for more extensive projects in the business sector. In 1974, the PIN was replaced by the Polamazonia project. The focus of attention was turned to cattle ranching, timber and mining interests. These were assisted by tax exemptions, land subsidies and fiscal incentives (Burns 1970). The scale and speed of Brazil's push for Amazonian integration continued to accelerate, rarely even taking the time to carry out basic preliminary studies to evaluate the feasibility of development plans. Input in the form of private investment and foreign loans to the government was treated as free fuel for conquering the Amazon; well-financed force and determination were given free rein to bring Amazonia under the plough, hoof and axe.

Ten to twelve years later, international banks began failing to see repayments on their Brazilian loans and a growing community of environmental and social protestors began petitioning the banks to cease funding for ill-planned development programmes. Institutions such as the World Bank began to review loan requests more carefully and to impose provisions for protective measures in the realization of the projects they funded. Everywhere where intensive "development" had been carried out, impoverished communities or abandoned lands were left behind as Brazil went on to its next project, apparently not reviewing the failures in its wake. The environmental conditions in Amazonia simply did not suit the forms of land use and occupation transplanted as models from the South. Colonists and construction crews routinely ran up against Indian communities previously uncontacted by the government's Indian agency. The processes of land exploitation escaped from government control in many areas, to be replaced by the governance of *pistoleiros*, or hired gunmen. Eventually, in order to secure further loans from international banks, Brazil had to implement specific reforms and guarantees for its Amazonian projects. Development began to proceed with more structure and paperwork, but to date it is doubtful that much has progressed with respect to environmental and social reforms. In fact, the more careful planning of development projects may have provided the opportunity for Brazil to begin systematizing its extermination of those aspects of the Amazon it found incompatible with the vision of a developed Brazil.

Moran (1983) characterizes the overall process of Amazonian industrial occupation as "growth without development". The businesses and infrastructures established in Amazonia have served ultimately to impoverish the region rather than to enrich it. The combination of foreign capital, extractive economies and unsuitability of forms of occupation imposed from outside the region have contributed to the resulting *underdevelopment* of the Amazon. The production strategies applied to Amazonia, while rarely benefiting their intended recipients outside the region, have systematically limited the opportunities for future internal development. The depletion of resources, decimation of local populations and knowledge systems, and the impoverishment of the soil/forest base have all acted to cripple Amazonia's ability to respond to viable future development opportunities. Local-level responses are now focusing on rehabilitating the ecological and social base for sustainability, rather than looking for the means to participate in national economic strategies. Yet government projects continue to exploit their areas of occupation, specifically for the purpose of advancing the national economy. In Amazonia, "the Brazilian strategy has clearly emphasized growth and put aside matters of equity" (Moran 1983).

The effective history of Amazonian development has created local awareness of the realities behind the government rhetoric. Opposition to the newest proposals for hydro-elecric energy is growing, although with some trepidation and fear, as Brazil has a history of internal repression and terrorism stemming from its military years. Under the democratic government that resumed in 1985, and its recently completed Constitution, there is hope that the people can begin to take risks and find support in official policy to resist colonization by national and foreign markets. It is during this time that the means the Brazilian people choose to ensure their rights will determine their relationships with the land, and within the economy and politics of the new state.

2. DAMS IN THE RAINFOREST: WHAT DO WE KNOW?

The ecology of tropical rainforest ecosystems has been the subject of extensive descriptions by naturalist explorers for nearly four centuries. The first accounts intended to relay information on the Amazon region were written in 1554, by the traveller and chronicler Carvajal. The lush appearance of the forest and diversity of life it supports had encouraged the assumption for many years that the soils of the tropical rainforest were extremely fertile. During his explorations in the 1800s, Henry Walter Bates wrote of the Amazon as "a region almost as large as Europe, every inch of whose soil is of the most exuberant fertility" (Stone 1985). Even after evidence began to show to the contrary (Wagley 1953), Theodore Roosevelt wrote of the region:

> When I consider the excessively small amount of labor
> required in this country, to convert the virgin forest into
> green meadows and fertile plantations, I almost long to come
> over with half a dozen friends, disposed to work, and enjoy
> the country; and show the inhabitants how soon an earthly
> paradise might be created.
>
> (Roosevelt 1919)

Meggers (1971) dispelled the myth of a rich soil base, calling the region a "counterfeit paradise" for its false appearance of fertility. Much of the Amazon rainforest actually subsists on a relatively poor soil foundation, the great majority of the system's nutrients being locked in the vegetation itself (Hecht 1985; Herrera 1985; Jordan 1985). This relatively recent understanding of rainforest ecology reflects our general *lack* of knowledge about tropical rainforests. Scientists are still identifying new species. Forest conditions and composition vary greatly within the Amazon rainforest. The complexities of "simple" relationships between rainforest species could take a lifetime to unravel. At present, our database is sorely insufficient to predict accurately the consequences of forest loss or the impacts of specific development projects. As tropical rainforest ecology becomes better understood, through much-needed research, more precise impacts can be detailed. However, at the rate at which we are now losing forestlands, there is great concern that little-known but very important interactions between tropical rainforests and vital global processes will be irreversibly damaged before they can be understood.

Extrapolating from the few available studies and projects, certain consequences of hydro-development have been noted which may have a serious impact upon tropical rainforest environments. This chapter reviews our current knowledge about rainforest systems as related to the effects of large dams. Few studies have been conducted on completed rainforest dams and the information which is available is general, or cursory at best. Further verification of the nature of the interactions and consequences will have to wait for the most recently constructed dams to reveal their effects. In Brazil, studies on the impacts of dams are conducted by the constructors, often pre-empting adequate research on the negative impacts. However, we do have some information to draw on in reaching a basic understanding of the environmental and human degradation associated with the large dam projects as they affect tropical rainforests.

Definition of tropical rainforests

Tropical rainforests (TRFs) occur in the Equatorial belt cutting across Central and South America, Asia, Africa, Australia and numerous Caribbean and Pacific Islands (see Figure 2.1). The Equatorial "green belt" refers to the band of tropical forest that lies along this line, mostly between the Tropic of Cancer and the Tropic of Capricorn, at 23.5

Figure 2.1: Distribution of tropical rainforests

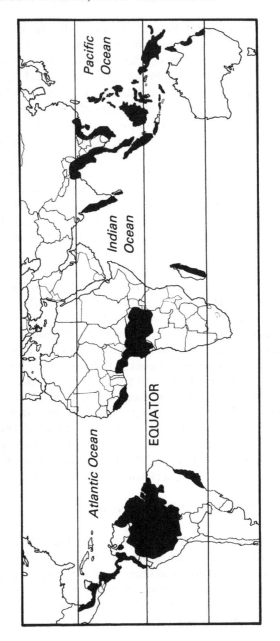

Source: Tasker 1987

degrees latitude North and South (Grainger 1980). This is the band in which the earth receives the maximum intensity of sunlight, crucial to the photosynthetic activity of the forest. Many scientists have identified a defining characteristic of TRFs as having an average temperature of 75+ degrees Fahrenheit (24+ Celsius) throughout the year (Myers 1984; Parsons 1975). The relative constancy of this temperature is critical to the constant growth conditions present in TRFs. Due to gradient temperature drops with increasing altitude, "true" TRFs are often considered as only lowland and low altitude tropical rainforest.

The most important defining characteristic of TRFs is clearly the amount of rainfall received in forest areas of the tropical zone. Myers (1984) cites 4,000 mm/yr as differentiating TRFs (sometimes called tropical moist forests) from seasonal or dry forests. To further classify TRFs as distinct from seasonal forests he suggests a rainfall requirement of at least 200 mm/month for 10 out of 12 months. The purpose of these clear definitions is to avoid applying descriptions of interactions of soils, rainfall and vegetation to anomalous forest types. These levels of rainfall result in a net excess of water, a determining factor in the proliferation of the biomass of tropical rainforests.

Additionally, it is important to define what is meant by primary tropical rainforest, as opposed to disturbed or previously cleared areas, termed secondary TRFs. Primary rainforest, used commonly in the scientific literature, refers here to forest communities which have been relatively undisturbed in recent years. Tree-fall gaps or low-impact use of standing forest are generally acceptable within this definition. It is doubtful that forests exist which have not been inhabited or disturbed at some point. "Primary" refers to a mature forest of native species, but avoids the implications of a "virgin", or untouched, ecosystem.

Tropical soils and dams

The soils of TRFs are largely ancient soils, impoverished through centuries of weathering and the leaching of essential nutrients. In Amazonia, more than three-quarters of the basin has soils of poor productive quality (Jordan 1985). Small patches of fertile deposits, with reasonable agricultural potential, are scattered throughout the basin. According to Myers (1984) only 4% are mature fertile soils. Approximately half of this area is represented by the annually inundated floodplains, traditionally among the most productive ecotypes of the forests (Meggers 1971). Other ecologists describe a more simplistic system. They differentiate two major types of soil-based communities: the *terra firma*, or inland forest, comprising 98% of Amazonia, and the *varzea*, or floodplain communities, being the 2% of the forest which is annually inundated during the rainy season and replenished with a top layer of sediment and nutrients (Fearnside 1985). These ecological communities are defined by distinct soil properties, forest composition and productive potential. It is the varzea which directly supported extensive native populations in large settlements, yet even here subsistence was integrated with a utilization of neighbouring forest types (Meggers 1971).

This two-tiered terra firma/varzea distinction has not proved sufficient to account for all observed differences in fertility and forest types. Using other criteria by which to differentiate the range of forest types occurring in the tropics, Tosi (1974) identifies 39 different "life zones" or bioclimates. While not all of these bioclimates would fit the description of TRF environments, his classification system highlights the complexity and variation too often ignored in the tropical forest zones.

The forest cover itself is built essentially on a thin layer of humus (decomposing leaf litter) covering the forest floor. It is here that virtually all of the ground nutrients are found, but only before they are quickly recycled into the vegetation (Stark and Jordan 1978). In most places, the average depth of the top humus layer is less than 10 cm (Lombana 1975). The nutrients vital for the growth of the forest only minimally reach the forest floor, with very little incorporation of the soil layer as a medium for the storage and uptake of nutrients. The great majority of the nutrients are contained in the plant biomass. One study of nutrient retention by forest vegetation was conducted in the poorest podzol soil forests of the Venezuelan Amazon. Here, Herrera (1985) found that 92% of the magnesium, 90% of the potassium, 74% of the calcium, 66% of the phosphorus and over 60% of the nitrogen in the system was contained in the plant biomass. When a large patch of forest is burned this vegetation is lost and the nutrients remaining in the ash are quickly removed with the topsoils during the first rains. Consequent leaching of the exposed subsoils completes the cycle of nutrient impoverishment (Lal 1987).

The thin layer of topsoil creates a great vulnerability to erosion when the forest cover is removed. The root systems of a standing forest act to hold the soil in place. Regional settlement and development in the areas of large dams often lead to the clearing of surrounding forestlands and expose the soil to the erosive force of the rains. An intact forest may lose only 1 ton of soil/hectare(ha)/year, which is naturally replenished. When the forest cover is removed, Grainger (1980) cites an increase in losses of 20–30 tons/year, conservative in comparison with Bunyard's (1985) average of 54 tons/year on cultivated soils. One study in humid tropical Nigeria has shown a loss of 55 tons of soil/ha in the first year and 35 tons in the second year on experimental bare fallow plots (Obi 1982).

In the area of large dams, eroded soils are often carried into the reservoir where siltation results. Concerning the Tucurui Dam in the Brazilian Amazon, Monosowski writes:

> Deforestation in the Tocantins watershed and the use of
> environmentally inappropriate cultivating techniques,
> particularly in commercial agriculture, cause increasing
> run-off. Run-off can erode the soil, exhaust soil fertility, and

lead to siltation and flooding. . . . On a long-term basis, the
water supply for the Tucurui reservoir could be affected by
these phenomena.

(Monosowski 1986)

Exactly this result affected the Anchicaya Project in the
Colombian Amazon. The dam experienced the loss of 80%
of its storage capacity in only 12 years due to siltation
of the reservoir (Allen 1972). The Ambuklao Dam in the
Philippines has had its operational life expectancy of 75
years reduced by more than a half due to siltation (Caufield
1982; Drucker 1985).

The trapping of annual soil deposits behind the barriers
of large dams has the additional effect of depriving the
riverbanks downstream of seasonal nutrient replenishment.

Quite apart from the ecological devastation it causes in the
area drowned by a dam's reservoir, impoundment prevents
a river's silt from being carried to the sea. That silt – which
generally contains large quantities of feldspar, clay, and
organic matter – often has a high nutrient value.

(Goldsmith and Hildyard 1984)

Communities or natural ecosystems downstream from the
dam are thus also threatened by the loss of topsoils to
reservoir sedimentation. Bondurant and Livesey (1973)
estimate that 25–75% of sediments normally carried
downstream will be lost, depending on the pattern of
controlled water releases. In addition to losing fertility,
the downstream riverbed is likely to suffer erosion as the
clear water released from the reservoir picks up sediments,
thus stripping the soils of the riverbanks (Glymph 1973).

Forest flooding and water cycles

Besides losing fertile silt deposits downstream, the absence
of natural annual inundation due to flood control by dams
disrupts the varzea communities, adapted to annual flood

cycles. Throughout the varzea floodplain, some fish feed on nothing but the seeds of the floodplain trees and play a vital role in the regulation of the ecosystem (Goulding 1985). With the alteration of the flood cycles caused by large dams, disruptions of these relationships could lead to widespread damage.

> Through their feeding activities, the fish help prepare nuts for germination; in addition, they distribute fruit seeds, which further assists the trees in return. As many as 200 fish and tree species appear to depend on each other and, of the fish, at least 50 are commercial species, making up three-quarters of the fish catch in Amazonia.
>
> (Myers 1984)

Disruption of the varzea system puts at risk not only the fauna and flora adapted to it, but also the regional economy and subsistence food production of the people who depend upon its productivity. In relation to the impacts on human subsistence, Barrow (1988) states: "Wildlife and people are adapted to flooding, even dependent upon it . . . smallholders in several riverside locations between [the Tucurui Dam] and a point about 60 km downstream . . . complained of the loss of cultivatable varzeas." The loss of the annual nutrient deposits and water-based oxygen reserves can disrupt the productivity of the forest for miles downstream.

The immediate area to be flooded can be plagued with several problems as a result of the failure to clear the standing forest before creation of the reservoir. This is becoming a common problem in Amazonia where neither the Tucurui nor Balbina Dams were cleared prior to flooding. The more resilient inundated timber decays only slowly, clogging the reservoir for many years. Decomposing vegetation causes eutrophication, an enrichment of the waters with nutrients, promoting algal growth and resulting in deoxygenation of the waters as the algae utilizes the available oxygen (Barrow 1988). The impacts include fish dying from suffocation and environmental damage to water-recipient areas downstream. At the Brokopondo Dam in Suriname, fish were found stunned by oxygen-deficient water 90 km downstream from the reservoir (Caufield 1982). The decomposition of the forest may also result in the build-up of hydrogen sulphide, polluting the waters and corroding the generating equipment. At one Brazilian dam, corrosion of equipment cost the constructors $5 million (Barrow 1988). The problems of deoxygenation, hydrogen sulphide and weed growth are also expected at Balbina by ecologists. In an attempt to find an alternative to the effort of clearing the forest at Tucurui, the power company (Eletronorte) used chemical defoliants, further polluting the water and reportedly resulting in the deaths of some employees from contamination. It is further suspected that some drums of the defoliant PCP (sodium pentachlorophenol) were lost under the waters of the reservoir (Barrow 1988). Finally, in 1989, an agreement was reached with Eletronarte for independent contractors to extract the submerged timber for private sale (Bryne 1989).

On a grander and poorly understood level of ecological interactions and regulation, the trapping of water in the formation of large reservoirs may affect the local climate. It has been reported that half of the Amazon basin's precipitation is recycled through transpiration from the forest plants and surface evaporation (Gat *et al.* 1985). While clear-felling tracts of rainforest disrupts this cycle and results in drying due to reduction in precipitation or interruption of rainfall cycles, it is not yet known what the effects of large reservoirs will be. Nemec (1973) reports that studies at Lake Michigan in the United States registered a 6% decrease in precipation over the water as compared with rainfall on land. However, other studies have shown opposite or neutral results, and Nemec stresses the importance of local meteorological studies in predicting the effects of reservoirs. It is important to recognize our lack of knowledge or comparable databases in determining climatological effects of large dam projects. As with many other aspects of altering tropical rainforest environments, our ignorance of the possible impacts may result in irreversible damage which threatens the viability of the original projects. Given the local drying trends and sedimentation rates indicated above, the operational lifespan of some rainforest dams may not even serve to pay back the costs of their construction.

Species losses to reservoirs

As with any development project which irreversibly alters its environment, flooding of large tracts of rainforest threatens the life of its plant and animal inhabitants. The diversity of plant and animal species occurring in the tropics is of a dimension we are just beginning to understand. While tropical biodiversity has been a major topic of recognition and study since before Darwin used species diversity to highlight evidence for his evolutionary theory, the extent of diversity in the tropics is just now coming to light. While ten years ago accepted numbers for the world's store of species ranged from 5 to 10 million (only 1.4 million of which have been named and a mere fraction of these studied (Wilson 1988)), estimates for insect species *alone* now reach 30 million (Erwin 1982). The vast majority of these are to be found in the tropics. The possibility that we may know of less than 5% of all species on earth points more than any other factor to the need for tropical rainforest research.

The prospect of losing such a great number of species to environmental mismanagement deserves some extra attention. Apart from the inherent value of diverse forms of life, the possible utility of these unknown species to human populations is likely to be high. For foods, medicines and commercial uses, the addition of some 5 million plant and animal species to our currently utilized natural resources would present a range of possibilities we cannot begin to predict.

Tropical rainforests occupy 7% of the earth's surface. Raven (1988) estimates that 66% of the world's species are found in TRFs, and half of these in Amazonia. Several theories attempt to explain the high diversity of TRF ecosystems. The age and stability (constancy) of the TRF environments have been credited with contributing a great deal to the proliferation of species diversity (Myers 1984). It is said that the constant conditions of the rainforest allow for new paths in creative evolution, unlikely to meet the limits imposed by more fluctuating environments in which species must be able to respond to regular changes in environment or location. Very specialized, localized species would thus have formed, responding only to specialized niche requirements in a system which has had perhaps 70 million years to develop a complex ecological network.

One of the favourite examples of these specialized relationships is offered by the sloths of Latin America's rainforests. Specifically adapted to live on the fur of the sloth are 3 species of beetles, 6 mites, 3 moths and even 3 types of algae (Caufield 1984). Large mammals are often the first victims of habitat disruption, acting as "indicator species" for the state of the ecosystem. If just this one mammal species were to suffer extinction due to forest destruction, its 15 dependent species would automatically be lost as well. The intricate complexities of TRF systems build upon subtle and far-reaching dependencies and co-relationships with other members of the forest community, lending to the diversity of its species components. The relationships are too complex to predict accurately all of the effects of habitat alteration. What we do not know about the roles affected species may play is likely to be more damaging than the effects we can foresee.

Another theory for TRF diversity focuses on the rarity and distribution patterns of many tropical species. Most members of one species are often widely scattered, presumably as a natural response in order to limit the proliferation of predatory or parasitic dependants. The resultant lack of domination of any one species type in an area has thus further opened opportunities for more species to evolve to fill the gaps, in a process termed *adaptive radiation*. The theory states that the result, in short, is a large number of rare species (Myers 1984), partially accounting for our lack of knowledge of TRFs. Studies on terra firma have shown that one square kilometre of TRF may boast a menagerie of 20–86 tree species, while inspection of an equal-sized stand of temperate forest may reveal only four species, each occurring repeatedly (Caufield 1984).

Explanations of high TRF diversity have often been based on theories related to geological change throughout a series of glacial eras. While many TRF species are found nowhere else on earth and others are found only in connection with certain hosts, many species are further isolated to small geographical areas, even if similar environments occur elsewhere. This phenomenon, referred to as *endemicity*, has been proposed to date back to events during a series of glacial eras. During the late Pleistocene era, periods of global cooling repeatedly caused the polar icecaps to expand, trapping a greater percentage of the earth's water reserves and causing a general drying trend. Similarly, during warmer phases the melting icecaps released water, leading to rising sea levels and increased precipitation. During the glacial phases, decreases in atmospheric water content reportedly limited rainfall around the Equatorial belt. In response, the tropical rainforests are said to have "shrunk", withdrawing to a few locations where conditions for survival were maintained (Prance 1985). These locations, called *refugia*, set the stage for the isolated evolution of some tropical rainforest species.

Refugia theory maintains that the effective islands of forest created by glaciations evolved in different ways and when they rejoined in the wetter interludes, each had developed new species unique to its geographical refugium. While certainly some of the more mobile species radiated to become common throughout TRFs, many remained unique to their places of origin. In this case, climatological disruptions in TRF stability increased, rather than limited, the biological diversity of these ecosystems. Using data of when the glacial periods occurred and censuses of regional levels of endemicity, refugia theorists are attempting to map the locations of several proposed refugia sites throughout the tropical forests. Salo (1986) suggests that diversity is higher along riverways due to the dynamic forest structures associated with constantly changing river channels. The diversity in resultant forest ecotypes and ages may lead to a greater range of species diversity in the varzea.

Whatever the explanation given for TRF diversity and endemicity, the bottom line when losing large tracts of rainforest is the likelihood of devastating impacts in terms of species losses and extinction. In the event of uninventoried tracts of forest being lost to flooding by large dams, the extent of these losses will probably never be known. All plants endemic to the area will be lost completely. Numerous studies are now being conducted revealing the many medicinal uses of rainforest plants (Arnason *et al.* 1980; Posey 1985). Even in mobile animal species which can escape the floods, populations will be diminished. For many TRF species which are already endangered, this could be the final step to extinction.

Goldsmith and Hildyard cite several examples of past dams' effects on endangered species:

> In North Perak, northern Malaysia, the Temengor Dam has drowned valuable forests, threatening the survival of 100 species of mammals and 300 species of birds. Most of these species are already near extinction. Most severely affected have been the Sumatran rhinoceros, the Malayan tapir, and the flying lemur.
>
> (Goldsmith and Hildyard 1984)

Here and elsewhere, the extinction of species is not only a wildlife problem: it also impacts upon the larger environment in unpredictable ways, and disrupts traditional forest and wildlife use by local peoples. Of the Tucurui Dam, Barrow (1988) states that, "Inevitably there have been species losses due to the construction", and cites threats to liana species, Brazil nut trees, the Tocantins River fish species, populations of manatee, river and Amazonian dolphin, turtle and cayman as examples of known cases in which the impact upon wildlife has been detrimental.

Dams and disease proliferation

Among the most obvious and direct effects of large dam construction is the increase in the incidence of disease in the local populations. With the creation of the reservoir:

> not only will animal and bird life be affected, but also plants,
> fungi, protozoa, bacteria and other micro-organisms. Many
> of those species play an integral part in the transmission
> of infectious diseases. It follows that as the composition
> of species in the new environment changes, so the pattern
> of disease will change also. Unfortunately, such change is
> usually for the worse. Indeed, in most cases, it has led to an
> upsurge in waterborne and other diseases.
>
> (Goldsmith and Hildyard 1984)

Common disease epidemics brought on by dam construction projects include malaria, schistosomiasis, onchocerciasis (river blindness) and indirectly gastroenteritis, respiratory and even venereal diseases. Additionally, Tucurui is threatened with Chagas disease (South American sleeping sickness) and bubonic plague (Barrow 1988).

The upsurge in malaria concurrent with the creation of artificial lakes has been recognized as a serious health hazard at least since the 1930s, when the Tennessee Valley Authority launched a number of projects in the United States (Brown and Deom 1973). In Amazonia, where malaria is highly endemic, it poses great risks to the health of local populations in almost every water development scheme. Malaria is transmitted by the *Anopheles* mosquito, whose prime breeding ground is wetlands or stagnant waters (Goldsmith and Hildyard 1984). The proliferation of *Anopheles* in artificial lakes combines with the sudden increase in human population attracted by the employment and development associated with the building of a dam.

The result is invariably an outbreak of malarial epidemics, worsened by the often poor health or lack of immunity of the affected populations (Hunter *et al.* 1982; Goodland 1986).

The building of large dams has resulted in an upsurge in the incidence of schistosomiasis, also found throughout the Amazon. The vectors of the disease are snails, in which the larvae of the schistosomes develop to infectious stage, and then enter through the skin of people bathing in contaminated waters (Goldsmith and Hildyard 1984). Even in areas where schistosomiasis was not previously known, as in the case of the Blue Nile, water impoundments have caused infection rates to rise as high as 70%, and up to 90% in schoolchildren (Amin 1979). Here, again, increased population combines with the formation of the snail's habitat to spread the disease even faster.

Another of the already present diseases worsened by concentration of habitat and people around a dam is river blindness, caused by the parasitic worm *Filaria*. Its prime breeding ground is fast-flowing water, such as the spillways of large dams (Goldsmith and Hildyard 1984). Following dam developments in the Volta River basin in Africa, 70,000 people contracted the disease and went blind. Several areas in Amazonia are also affected.

Overcrowded conditions and poor sanitation are indirect consequences of any large development project open to population influxes in Amazonia. Poor preparation or disregard for these effects around dams has resulted in unhealthy conditions leading to pneumonia, gastro-intestinal diseases, hepatitis, tuberculosis and even high incidence of gonorrhoea and syphilis (Goldsmith and Hildyard 1984).

Hydro-development and indigenous peoples

A discussion of traditional settlement in the Amazon basin is a necessary component for an integrated understanding of the effects large development projects have had on the total environment, including its indigenous peoples. Evidence now indicates that human settlement in the region may be as much as 14,000 years old (Meggers 1971). In connection with Amazonia's people, as with its soils, past and present statements by travellers and students are laden with gross misconceptions. Among the first of these is that the aboriginal Amazonian is a primitive race, subsisting largely on a diet of meat, or even human remains. This view was propounded not only by ignorant, fearful settlers, but also by some early anthropologists who focused only on the "interesting", exotic characteristics of their societies, and exaggerated rare or ritualistic behaviours. Following this, and still widely accepted among people who have had little or no contact with the Indian people, came the magnanimous, paternalistic opinion that the Amazonian natives were innocent, eager and childlike.

The Church began to work intensively to convert the Indians to Christianity. At this stage it was believed that the indigenous peoples simply lacked technology, religion and perhaps a little intelligence, but that they could be raised to the "level" of the European colonizers. Rather than learn from the native peoples, the colonists chose to teach them the "right way". It was assumed that they had no knowledge or technology worth the interest of "civilized" peoples. Yet, crucial to the European's success in surviving the Amazon environment, the indigenous people provided a labour force and, despite cultural biases against their "inferiority", held crucial knowledge such as which plants could cure the colonists' illnesses.

The government which has come to power in Brazil today still holds this basic view of the Indian. An Indian agency has been created to integrate the Indians into Brazilian society and bring to them the benefits of "civilization". The state assumes the role of guardian and mentor for the "relatively incapable" Indian peoples (Brazilian Constitution 1966). To the contrary, modern anthropologists are reporting astonishing levels of complexity in the social organization and agricultural practices of the Amazonians (Posey 1985).

Recent reports of their extensive knowledge of forest plants, constituting virtual medicinal storehouses, have dispelled the impression of their use of "folk" remedies as being superstitious magic (Anderson and Posey 1987; Plotkin 1988). It is becoming impossible to deny the vast superiority native Amazonians have over colonizers when it comes to living in the forest. Not just in adaptation, but in technology and knowledge, forms of forest use by native peoples are proving more suitable to Amazonia's lands, and much more complex than previously imagined.

In one study, Posey (1985) has shown that the Kayapo of the Xingu river region (the Xingu is a major tributary of the Amazon) intensively manage their forest for the benefit of their own purposes. In a survey conducted in 1983, only 2 of 140 plants collected by scientists from the forest were not considered useful by the Kayapo. Furthermore, they identified 85% of the useful plants as having been planted by themselves. Posey estimates that in areas of indigenous habitation, as much as 75% of forest once considered "natural" is in fact the result of human intervention and management. Among the uses for which the Kayapo "create" their forests are food, medicines, tools, firewood, trade and ceremonial goods, disease reduction, shelter, and attraction of birds and game. Posey states:

> It becomes clear that the Kayapo view forest management
> as an integrated system of plant communities rather than
> individual species; likewise, manipulated wildlife and even
> semi-domesticated bees figure into the overall management
> strategies. The long term management strategies of the
> Kayapo, which actually increase species diversity, offer
> many fundamental principles that should guide development
> throughout the humid tropics along a path that is both
> ecologically and socially sound.
>
> (Posey 1985)

With the continuation of these types of studies we may finally begin to understand the nature of traditional human ecology in the tropical rainforests.

These same Kayapo serve as an example of native populations threatened by construction plans for hydroelectric dams in the Amazon. The Xingu Dams Complex will flood portions of the forest communities referred to in Posey's study, as well as the villages of many of the Kayapo who contributed to the research. In other areas of Amazonia, numerous people have been relocated or placed at government posts in order to make way for reservoirs intended to generate electricity for Brazil's urban centres and industrial complexes. At the Tucurui Dam, which supplies energy for the Grande Carajas Project (largely a mining operation), the flooding of the reservoir encroached on three Indian reserves, forcing the removal of 800 people from 6 tribal groups (Monosowski 1986). Impacts of relocation and social upheaval are not limited to the indigenous populations. Tucurui also displaced 15,000 people from Brazilian towns and villages, many of whom did not receive due compensation.

While the impacts of loss of land and livelihood, as well as relocation, are devastating for Indians and Brazilians alike, the Indian people run the additional risk of widespread exposure to diseases to which they have not developed immunity. They are also threatened with relocation to posts or reserves where they cannot support themselves and must rely on insufficient or corrupt government agencies for the necessities for survival. The value in human lives, cultures and scientific knowledge necessary in many cases for our own survival in and out of the forests, makes this consequence of dam construction and other forms of development one of the most devastating of the "costs" suffered. In recent cases, attempts by the Kayapo and other Indians to negotiate terms or oppose dams and other development projects have been firmly rejected (Kaiapo 1988a; Terena 1988).

3. THE 2010 PLAN

Brazil's plans for energy production to the year 2010 have been detailed in the government's "2010 Plan". Released in 1987, the Plan covers Brazil's proposed energy development programmes from that year. The focus of the Plan is to supply energy for Brazil by utilizing the country's hydroelectric potential, the great majority of which is concentrated in the Amazonian rivers. The Amazon is seen as the source for Brazil's increasing industrialization; the provider of the electric energy which will make possible the country's continued development.

Eletrobras, the national power company, describes the Brazilian energy system as being characterized by a great hydrological potential. It recognizes with this certain associated characteristics of Brazil's proposed energy system: the diversity in the character and quality of the regions it plans to utilize; the need for the creation of large reservoirs; and the requirement of long-distance transmission lines, as the centres of production are far from the main centres of demand or consumption (Eletrobras 1987, p.55).[1] The viability studies conducted prior to each project are designed to take these general characteristics into account. Eletrobras considers these studies as an informational base from which financing negotiations can be made. A number of environmental guidelines have been designed to lessen the negative impacts of the characteristics of the Brazilian energy programme.

The 2010 Plan outlines 31 hydroelectric dams (*usina hidrelétricas* – UHEs) to be constructed in the northern region (not including the already completed Balbina and

Figure 3.1: Amazonian dams – proposed, in construction and completed

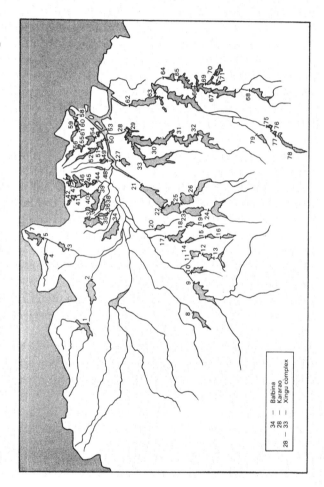

34 — Balbina
28 — Kararaô
28 – 33 — Xingu complex

Source: CPI 1988

Tucurui Dams).[2] While the Plan makes no further mention of other projects, previous documents have revealed plans for the eventual construction of 79 dams on the Amazon's tributaries (Santos and Andrade 1988) (see Figure 3.1). The entire country will play a role in the hydroelectric energy production to be attained, but the concentration of activity will be centred in the North.

Nine of the ten hydroelectric dams listed that will produce more than 2,000 megawatts (MW) will be located in the North. The total potential for hydroelectric energy production to be installed in this region is estimated at 72,822 MW (p. 152–8). The firm (guaranteed) energy projected is just under 40,000 MW.

As of 1988, few large works in Amazonia had yet reached the reservoir stage. Tucurui, in Para, had flooded an area of 2,430 km[2], and Balbina had inundated 2,346 km[2]. The reservoir of the Samuel Dam was filled in 1989. Only Tucurui has been put into operation. The 2010 Plan predicts that by the year 2000, implemented projects will create reservoirs inundating 0.3% of Amazonia, or 1.6 million hectares (p. 150). However this includes only the first 4 of the North's 31 projected hydro-projects, and may not include Balbina or Tucurui. Other estimates project that the entire programme through to 2010 will claim approximately 5% of Amazonia's lands, an area greater than the size of Montana (Deudney 1981).

Brazil expects that the country's energy demand will increase fourfold by 2010. 1985 estimates projected a demand for 211.7 Terawatt hours (1 Terawatt hour (TWh) = the power produced by 1 million Megawatts in an hour) in 1988, rising to a need for 680.1 TWh to meet consumption in 2010 (p. 42). Less than 10% of the demand, approximately 65 TWh, is expected to arise in the North. Yet the 2010 Plan outlines a system of hydroelectric dams in the North that would produce over 45% of the nation's electrical energy needs here (p. 43, 62) (see Table 3.1).

The major increases in electricity demand will come from the need to supply Brazil's increasing industrialization.

Table 3.1: Energy production* and consumption 1986–2010 (% by region)

	1986		*2010*	
	Production	*Consumption*	*Production*	*Consumption*
North	4.8	5.3	58	10
Northeast	13.2	13.2	6	16
South	13.1	13.7	16	18
Southeast/ Centrewest	52.4	67.8	20	56

* Production refers only to hydroelectric energy. Estimates are based on production *potential*.

Source: *2010 Plan*, Eletrobras 1987; pp. 43, 56, 152–6

Eletrobras's projections expect industry to account for 57.5% of the increase in demand by the year 2010 (p. 44). This estimate is based on extrapolations of energy-use patterns for 1985. Ninety per cent of Brazil's energy consumption in 1985 was accounted for by four categories of use (p. 33): *industry* consumed 56% of national energy production; 20% of consumption was attributed to *residential* use (presumably primarily urban); 11% of use was accounted for by *commercial* utilization; and only 3% of the energy consumption was attributed to *rural* forms of electricity usage. It is difficult to determine exactly what types of activities these varying consumptions of electricity refer to, as definitions of the categories are not offered in the Plan. It is not clear what the forms of rural energy use are apart from residential, or what constitutes "commercial" use. However, it is fairly clear that industrial use refers to the transformation of materials and production-orientated activity, rather than individual or low-level utilization.

In 1986, 66% of the national energy supply was consumed in the Southeast (p. 43). The majority of this region's energy is consumed by industry. Similarly, the Northeast and Southern regions' energy consumptions, which are also greater than the North's, are attributable largely to industry. The Northeast uses 59% of its energy consumption in industry, and the South attributes 48% of its electricity use to industrial forms. The Southeast portrays the nation's imbalances in production and consumption centres. Supplying 51% of production, the Southeast consumed 66% of the nation's energy in 1986. Thus, 15% of the energy it used was produced in another region. With plans for 45% of the country's generation potential to be installed in the North, and only 10% of demand expected to stem from here in 2010, the imbalances will grow greater, creating an energy extraction scenario where the North will be exploited to support the industries of the South and Northeast regions (see Figure 3.2).

The total potential to be installed in the country by 2010 is 141.8 GW (1 gigawatt (GW) = 1,000 million watts), up from 38.5 GW in 1986 (p. 144). The North has the greatest potential for hydro-power development, owing to the great energy potential of the Amazonian rivers. It is estimated that 45.4% of the nation's potential in hydroelectric energy is in the North, as compared with 15.8% in the South, 7.7% in the Northeast, and 31.1% in the Southeast and Centre-west combined (p. 62). The 2010 Plan outlines a programme to tap 78% of the North's inventoried and economically available firm energy, or a total of 28.2 GW/year (p. 145).

The plans of Eletrobras show that by 2010, 47% of the Northeast's electricity will be imported from the North. 26% of the energy consumption of the Southeast and Centre-west will be imported from the northern region (p. 147). The energy required by the industrial centres of the country to maintain their growth and development rates will be extracted from Amazonia. The North could be self-sustaining with small, appropriate hydro-projects. In order to supply the demands of the rest of the nation,

Figure 3.2: Inter-regional electricity flux – firm energy (MW/year)

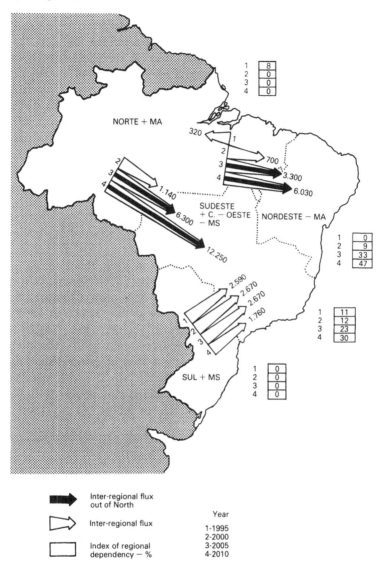

Source: Eletrobras 1987

Brazil plans a utilization of its energy resources to fuel an economy outside Amazonia. The plans also require the installation of long-distance transmission lines for the export of electricity from the North to Brazil's industrial centres, some over 2,800 km long. The transfer of electricity to the Northeast will be facilitated by transmission lines of around 1,500 km in length. Transportation of energy to the southern regions will be an even greater feat. One line of 2,300 km, three lines of 2,400 km, and two lines each of 2,600 km and 2,800 km will be necessary for this transfer of electricity from the North to the South (p. 159) (see Figure 3.3). While Eletrobras fails to discuss the efficiency of this programme, or to consider the results of studies concerning energy losses in long-distance transmission, it does make reference to the financial costs of its transmission plans. The 2010 Plan estimates that the lines will require an investment of $10–12/MWh, plus an additional $3/MWh in losses (p. 108). The document does not go into discussion on this matter but it seems to indicate that Brazil expects a 25–30% loss of energy in its long-distance transmission.

One example of an early hydroelectric project planned to produce electricity for "export" use is the Kararao Dam, on the Xingu River, a tributary of the Amazon. Kararao is expected to begin producing energy in 1999, initially at an output of 2,200 MW. The first year of generation will see the transmission of electricity to the Northeast. During the second year (2000), additional power will be exported to São Paulo, a distance of 2,600 km southwest (p. 169).

Eletrobras points out the positive aspects of developing its hydro-power potential. Hydroelectricity is seen as a renewable energy source, and the reservoirs and works created in utilizing its capacity can be used for many other purposes, such as drinking and irrigation water. Significantly, its other justification and "positive aspect" is the nation's extensive experience with hydroelectric constructions; thus the great potential of the country can be tapped with reasonable technical autonomy (p.61).

Figure 3.3: North to South transmission

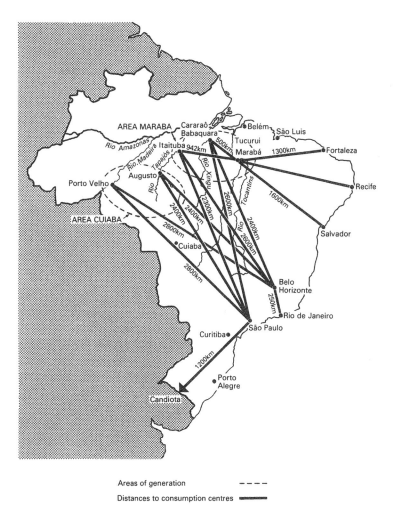

Areas of generation ----
Distances to consumption centres ▆▆▆▆

Source: Eletrobras 1987

Eletrobras claims: "The country meets a sufficiently developed level of professional training in the area of design and construction of hydroelectric dams" (p. 243).

However, this analysis overlooks three critical points. First, the concept of hydro-power as a renewable energy source can only hold true if the works are successful and efficient enough to continue generation over a long period of time. The experiences with other hydroelectric works in areas ecologically similar to those planned for Amazonia have a history and a reputation for failing or silting up long before their expected life span is reached (Allen 1972; Drucker 1985).

Second, the claim of extensive national experience does not apply to the development of hydroelectric schemes in the region in which the Plan concentrates its attention. The northern region, mostly the Amazonian basin rainforest, is a vastly different environment to the regions where Brazil has had most of its experience in the construction of hydroelectric dams. At the time when the Plan was released in 1987, Eletronorte, the northern subsidiary of Electrobras, had not had the opportunity to complete and study the effects of a single one of its large hydroelectric projects. Tucurui had just been completed, but impact studies following its construction had not been conducted. Studies which had been conducted at Tucurui before and during its construction are not particularly favourable (Goodland 1986; Monosowski 1986). Post-construction reports on Tucurui describe disastrous social and environmental effects (Caufield 1984; Barrow 1988). The Balbina Dam's reservoir had not even been filled at the time the 2010 Plan was written, but it is widely acknowledged that the project is a disaster and a "mistake", due to excessive economic, environmental and social costs (Pimenta-Neves 1989; *New York Times* 1989a).

Finally, the statement that Brazil can carry out its hydro-power development plan without foreign technical assistance is overshadowed by the fact that the country must borrow large sums of money, as it cannot realize the Plan without extensive foreign financial assistance.

Currently, Brazil's foreign debt is $116 billion, and inflation has exceeded 25% per month. Between 1987 and 1991, the average annual investment in developing the 2010 Plan will amount to $6.4 billion. In the following five years, 1992–6, this figure will rise to $7.5 billion/year (p. 200). The financial assistance Brazil will require in loans may further cripple its economy, especially if the projections for hydroelectric energy production overestimate the realistic success with which the plan can expect to meet.

Notes

1. Page numbers appearing alone refer to the 2010 Plan.
2. Most discussion will refer to figures including Balbina and Tucurui, unless otherwise noted.

4. BALBINA: A CASE STUDY

Before initiation of the 2010 Plan, Brazil had already had experience in building large hydroelectric projects. In the North, however, this experience was limited and, many say, disastrous. Two of the largest projects in Amazonia are the Tucurui and Balbina Dams. Eletronorte's claim of having a "sufficiently developed level of training" in hydroelectric works is not supported by the illustration of these two projects.

This chapter will cover the history and development of the Balbina Dam in Amazonas (discussions on the Tucurui Dam have been presented by Goodland (1978), Monosowski (1986) and Barrow (1988)). Balbina is particularly insightful as it represents one of the earliest hydroelectric projects to be initiated, yet is still in the construction stage. The limits on design and implementation capacity are thus highlighted, as well as its long history of poor environmental and social policy. Details of regional development history and the hydroelectric dam itself are reviewed, followed by a discussion of local and international responses.

History

The Balbina Dam is located 146 km north of the city of Manaus, on the Uatuma River. With a generating potential of only 250 megawatts (MW), the reservoir floods an area of approximately 2,346 km^2. The majority of the region was relatively undisturbed rainforest until 1970. A portion of the area inundated by the reservoir had been recently designated as the Waimiri-Atroari Reserve. The dam is only one of several development projects which have entered on to these lands in the past 20 years. At a current cost of $700 million dollars, Balbina represents the most expensive and poorly designed of the Brazilian dams to date. Yet the non-financial costs of the dam and its concurrent regional development projects represent the even greater price that has been paid by the local people, most of whom will receive none of the benefits.

Rather than being turned away on my visit to the national power company's central offices in Brasilia, as expected, Eletronorte arranged for me a first-class tour to the dam and accommodation during the length of my stay there. I had only to explain that I was an American researcher interested in Brazil's progress in hydroelectric development. My first view of Balbina was from the window of the government plane in which we arrived at the site. The central mass of the concrete barricade could be seen above the tree line from miles away. The area around the dam had been cleared. After an hour-long flight over continuous rainforest canopy, cut by the winding channel of the Uatuma River, we angled down into the swathe of brown extending from the dam site and the government village. We were escorted without words to the chief engineer's office. "Chefe" Queiroga welcomed us brusquely and launched into a tirade against environmentalists who had criticized Balbina, to assure us that they were unjust. At the end of his speech, all of the criticisms suffered by the project were summarized as the fault of Rachel Carson and her writing of *The Silent Spring*, a book concerned with the environmental impact of industrial factories in the United States. This introduction to Balbina was followed by my first view of the site on an official grand tour. Later, I would return with a social-work team for an extensive view of the problems of the dam and the surrounding region.

The history of this region of northern Amazonia is valuable in understanding the effects of government development policy. Construction on the Balbina Dam began in 1981. Previously, regional infrastructure projects had been established for this and other development programmes to be introduced into the area. As recently as 1970, access to

Table 4.1: Waimiri-Atroari population decline

Year	Population	Source
1905	6,000	Georg Hubner and Koch-Gruenberg
1968	3,000	Joao Calleri/Prelazia de Roraima
1972	3,000	FUNAI
1974	600/1,000	Gilberto Pinto Figueredo
1982	571	Guiseppe Craveiro/FUNAI
1983	350	Stephen Baines

Source: Jordan 1987, p. 15

the forest area to the north of Manaus was limited to the river and trade relationships with the Indian inhabitants. The major group in this region, the Waimiri-Atroari, had been contacted long before by explorers and traders along the rio Negro and rio Branco, and undoubtedly less favourably by rubber barons and slave traders. Their original population, before European contact, is estimated to have been 6,000 (MAREWA 1987). Epidemics of diseases introduced by the Europeans and direct conflict in the early years of colonization reduced their number by half, leaving a population of 3,000 (see Table 4.1). By 1970 this population had stabilized and was involved in trade relationships with the city of Manaus on the Amazon River to the south.

In July 1971, President Medici announced the creation of the Waimiri-Atroari Reserve (decree no. 68.907/71 (03)) (see Figure 4.1). The reserve was placed in the forest area directly north of Manaus. The traditional lands of the Waimiri-Atroari covered an area of 8,000,000 hectares (ha). The reserve limited their lands to 1,146,100 ha, a little less than 15% of their original lands (Schwade, in print). Yet,

Figure 4.1: Waimiri-Atroari Reserve

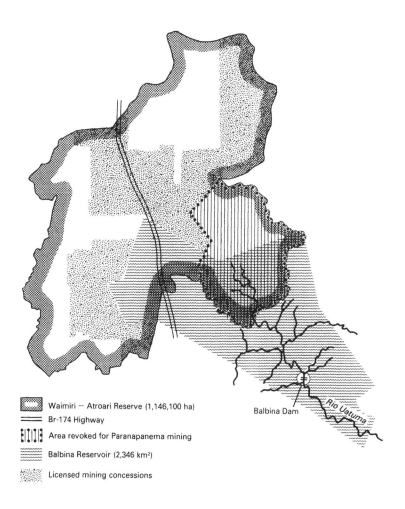

Waimiri — Atroari Reserve (1,146,100 ha)

Br-174 Highway

Area revoked for Paranapanema mining

Balbina Reservoir (2,346 km²)

Licensed mining concessions

Balbina Dam

Rio Uatuma

the reserve was presumably intended to provide protection for the Waimiri-Atroari and to protect against encroachment by regional settlement and development. All the remaining population was moved into the designated area. The government Indian agency FUNAI (National Indian Foundation) established posts within the reserve for the purposes of providing assistance with resettlement, food aid and medical services. However, the events following these "protective" measures resulted in the greatest threats and losses yet to affect the Waimiri-Atroari. FUNAI was enlisted to prepare the Indians for the coming invasion of their lands.

Immediately after the creation of the Waimiri-Atroari reserve, the BR–174 highway was scheduled to bisect the area directly (see Figure 4.1). BR–174 is part of the Transcontinental Highway, linking Brasilia with Venezuela. The highway was planned and initiated from Brasilia in 1968, prior to the creation of the reserve, yet plans for its path through the reserve area were not announced until after the Indian land was decreed. Throughout 1974, attempts by FUNAI to "pacify" and encourage the Indians to accept the road failed, but the government persisted with its plans. Today, the road is functional only in dry weather, rarely allowing passage along its full length. At all times of the year, travel is rough, as I learned too well during a ride hitched from the town of Presidente Figueredo, near the reserve, to Manaus. I, another traveller, and a roped bull shared the back of a flat-bed truck, leaving the lot of us tangled, sore and covered with hay and bull spittle at the end of the two-hour journey.

During construction of the famous highway, wars broke out between the Waimiri-Atroari and construction crews, and the Waimiri-Atroari and FUNAI. On 27 December 1974, the regional director of FUNAI, Gilberto Pinto Figueredo, was killed in an attack on the Abonari Indian post (Davis 1977). His replacement, Sebastião Amancio, announced a new strategy to be implemented in the Waimiri-Atroari Reserve.

Amancio planned to build a fort where the last attack on Figueredo had occurred and equip it with one entrance, an emergency ladder, a stock of dynamite, gas bombs, machine guns and grenades, as "a demonstration of the force of our civilization" (Davis 1977). With the resultant outcry from the press and the public, FUNAI announced that Amancio would be suspended pending an investigation of his remarks. Fifteen years later, my visit to Manaus revealed that Amancio still retains the post of regional director and his approach to the indigenous people has changed little since the time of his appointment. Official and unofficial policy in the Waimiri-Atroari Reserve reflects Amancio's influence. In 1985, members of the remaining Waimiri-Atroari tribe asked missionaries working within the reserve: "What is it that *Kamna* [civilization] throws from the airplane and forest at our people?", "Why does *Kamna* kill our people?" The substance thrown from the planes, a powder, reportedly burned their throats and resulted in immediate death (Schwade, in print).

Before Figueredo's death, he reported that by 1974 the population of the Waimiri-Atroari had dropped to between 600 and 1,000, a reduction of at least 66% in only two years, since the construction of BR–174 had begun. In addition to deaths by direct warfare, the influx of disease with the opening of the road further decimated the population at record speed. No accounts are available for the incidence of disease among the Waimiri-Atroari with the building of the road, but similar experiences elsewhere illustrate the devastating rise in diseases alongside road-construction projects. *Anopheles* mosquitoes normally inhabit the canopy, but with forest felling the malarial vectors are forced to the ground and subsequently thrive on the increased human populations in areas of high development activity. With the building of the Transamazon Highway, the prevalence of malaria increased between 150 and 1,200% in settlements near the road in the states through which it passed (Hunter *et al.* 1982).

Despite resistance, the construction of the BR–174

highway was finished in 1977 but allowed only daytime traffic in armed convoys (Schwade, in print). The road, intended for military access to the border and for access to mineral reserves in the North, also opened the Waimiri-Atroari area to further development. In 1975, a site bordering the reserve was recommended for the hydroelectric scheme of Balbina (Eletronorte, undated) (see Figure 4.1). In the following years, technical and preparatory studies were carried out.

Large- and medium-scale mining operations have been established in the reserve. The mining firm of Paranapanema opened the northeastern block of the reserve to mineral exploration in 1979 (Jordan 1987), (see Figure 4.1). Following this, the area was revoked by decree no. 86.630 for an extensive mining operation, and a city has since been built on the site to support these activities. The position of other mineral projects operating within the reserve is less clear. Over half of the remaining area has been licensed to various mining subsidiaries, but remains legally demarcated reserve (CEDI 1987), (see Figure 4.1).

Once the regional infrastructure and "ground-breaking" was established, the path was opened for the implementation of the government's plans for the Balbina hydroelectric project. The dam serves as an example of the extensive ramifications large development projects can deliver to a region, and the imbalances in political power which permit these events. The creation of a reservoir of 2,346 km^2 was expected to generate 250 MW, enough to supply the city of Manaus at the time the project was initiated. The flat topography of the region required a reservoir of extensive size to generate even a minimal amount of energy (Tucurui flooded a slightly smaller area for the production of 8,000 MW). Today, Manaus has grown to consume much more than Balbina's generating capacity, and an additional hydro-power project is being constructed to supply the difference. From the beginning, the inefficiency and negative impacts of Balbina were predicted, yet the project proceeded as a monument to the developmental and industrial capacity of a new Amazon.

At the time construction of the Balbina Dam began in 1981, less than 600 Waimiri-Atroari remained. The portion of the reserve planned for inundation was dismembered by FUNAI as an "area temporarily interdicted", a new term introduced in their official documents by decree no. 85.989 (MAREWA 1987). By 1983, with yet more pressure on their lands and a greater influx of disease into the area, the Waimiri-Atroari population fell to 350 people.

The dam was scheduled for operation in 1987. Yet it was not until this same year that relocation arrangements were finally made for the people of Taquari and Tapupuna, the two villages to be flooded by the reservoir (Eletronorte/FUNAI 1988). The people to be relocated constituted a third of the surviving population. New posts were established by FUNAI for their resettlement. Throughout the reserve, several relocated communities have been settled along the BR–174. One of these posts is so close to the road that anybody driving through can stop and enter the village, which is common practice for buses travelling from Manaus to Boa Vista (Chernela 1988). The Waimiri-Atroari are now dependent on government provisions for their food, clothing and health care, unable themselves to provide for their basic needs.

Looking beyond the effects that Balbina has had on the indigenous people reveals the dissatisfaction of many Brazilians with the implications of the project. For some, the reasons are personal – communities of peasant farmers lost their lands just as the Waimiri-Atroari did. For others, as within the universities or more critical government agencies in Manaus, the reasons for protest are based largely on environmental or economic grounds. The lands flooded by the dam represented largely intact, primary rainforest. The economic costs involved have run so far to $700 million.

Thirty-two miles downstream from Balbina, the riverine community of Cachoeira Morena was seriously affected by the dam. The river had provided the community with food (through fishing and small floodplain agricultural gardens), drinking water, sanitation and transportation. In 1987, when the floodgates were closed, these means of subsistence were entirely disrupted. Eletronorte established a social-service programme to relocate and rehabilitate the families affected. Forty-two families, totalling 350 people, were involved (Lange 1988). The social-work team responsible for this programme invited me to join them at one of the meetings of the union representing the displaced communities. The families had been settled on new lands inland from the river, and a road was cut through the area to provide passage and transportation. Most of the families have no means of land transport. *En route* to the meeting site, the half-sized pickup truck I travelled in stopped frequently until it carried more than 25 people. At one point, I was deposited at the side of the road, to wait "until the next car comes along". Everybody managed, however, to arrive at the site. Their livelihood depended on the strength of their union.

The families were expected to farm their small plots to grow enough food for themselves, and eventually for commercial sale to the village of Balbina. Very few plots have provided even minimal subsistence. The efforts required to establish a productive garden some distance from the road, where the soil has not been damaged, is too great an input for so unstable and tentative a community. The people of Morena have not received legal title to their new lands and, without the security of land ownership, the families are unlikely to invest in production. The Rural Agricultural Workers' Union is currently attempting to solve this problem. In order to survive under the new conditions, many of the relocated people are now employed as wage labourers for the construction of Balbina, or rely on market trade with the government village in order to support their families. Similar to the situation of the Waimiri-Atroari, the riverine peoples can no longer provide for their basic needs without reliance on the government programmes (Rural Agricultural Workers' Union, 1988).

One form of assistance provided by Eletronorte was the provision of materials to build wells, as a substitute for the loss of water from the river. While not all of the functions of the river are replaced through the use of wells, it has at least provided a source of drinking water. Closer to the dam site, where scattered houses have remained on the river banks, the wells provided by Eletronorte will be submerged when the dam begins operation and a greater volume of water flows again in the riverbed. At this time the quality of the river water will be unsuitable for drinking. The flow will be drained from the bottom of the reservoir and will be lacking in oxygen, as well as having been passed through the generating turbines and machinery of the hydroelectric plant. Here, the people expect Eletronorte to build them new wells when the water rises, and to continue to provide a market for the new forms of production they have adopted in response to the presence of the busy government town.

Characteristic of large hydro-development projects, Balbina has had serious repercussions on the fauna and flora of the forest ecosystem. An area of at least 2,346 km^2 of tropical rainforest has been flooded for the production of electricity and few definitive impact studies of the project have been conducted, let alone released. The explanations for this are varied. First, the project is not yet complete, thus a full study of the environmental effects is not yet possible. More importantly, all research on the impacts of government projects is conducted through the governmental research agencies. Known effects are sometimes withheld from public knowledge, while other studies are never allowed to be carried to completion (Fearnside 1988). The priorities of Eletronorte lie not in the monitoring of the environment, but in the production of electricity, and relatively few of its resources are invested in determining the environmental effects of development projects. However, general effects of large-dam construction have been reviewed by Goldsmith and Hildyard (1984) and can be extrapolated to the Balbina hydroelectric dam.

The majority of the forest inundated by the reservoir

was not cleared prior to filling, and the resulting anaerobic decomposition of the forest biomass pollutes the water supply and increases the acidity of the water. Deoxygenation further affects aquatic and riverine flora and fauna within the reservoir and in the affected areas downstream. More fundamentally, the wasted timber represents a vast resource of great value. Yet these effects do not override Eletronorte's consideration of the investment in forest clearing as uneconomical. The extent and speed at which the Amazonian forests are presently being logged for timber makes it difficult to justify the drowning of such an extensive area while ignoring the timber reserves which will consequently be cut from other forest tracts.

The flooding of any large area of tropical rainforest carries with it the likelihood of losing great resources of wildlife and flora, including entire species which may be endemic to the region. In the case of Balbina, Eletronorte has established an environmental "wildlife salvage" programme. During the filling of the reservoir, teams of workers scout the drowning forest islands for trapped wildlife which has failed to escape. In general, the majority of their rescues are of turtles and monkeys, occasionally making way for the retrieval of snakes and sloths. These "salvages" are then transported to a biological reserve area identified by the project, and released. On one side the reserve is bordered by the nearly dry riverbed, clearly a disturbed condition likely to have an impact on the ability of the forest to support even its original wildlife populations. No studies of re-adjustment or possible overcrowding of the reserve area in relation to its carrying capacity have been attempted.

It is quite common for animals to be injured or killed in the course of transportation and release (fieldnotes, 1988). The salvage employees are unskilled in wildlife handling and have been observed to neglect injured animals or mistreat individuals that are to be transferred. As I watched one of these release operations, an adult howler monkey was forceably separated from her infant while being removed from the holding cage. The infant was dropped on to her back as she ran from the cage, along a cut swath of road. Frightened by brutal handling, she ran up the nearest tree, too small to support her weight. The salvage workers threw rocks to frighten her down. She dropped the infant to the ground and jumped to the next tree. The 40-foot fall broke the infant's back, but was not immediately fatal. As I was leaving, the salvage team was taking a lunch break, leaving the infant to lie on top of the cages. Hours later it appeared in the veterinary clinic for treatment, but died soon after.

In June 1988, members of the National Institute for Amazon Research (INPA) were planning a search expedition in an area soon to be flooded. A new bird species had been found in a small region planned for inundation and INPA wanted to find and catalogue the species before the area was flooded (Conhaft 1988). If found, it was possible that a pair could be relocated elsewhere. The alternative was extinction, perhaps one of the first to be definitively recorded as the result of a specific development project.

The abundance of disease vectors in the area of Balbina may have increased with the construction of the dam; the closest town to the project, Presidente Figueredo, suffered from epidemics of malaria and leishmaniasis (caused by a subcutaneous parasite). During my visit, a town resident related that the assistance extended by Eletronorte consisted of a single round of vaccinations for the inhabitants, all given in one day, and not until after many people were already ill. By contrast, the government employees at Balbina received extensive medical preparation and have ready access to the project's well-stocked hospital. Malaria now appears to have been eradicated in the immediate vicinity of the dam as a result of thorough treatment programmes.

The effects on the environment downstream from Balbina are equally disruptive. The repercussions that have required the relocation of the community of Cachoeira Morena represent a devastating impact on local fish populations as well as on the entire varzea community, which is likely to be damaged by more than two years' interruption of the annual flood cycles. Varzea ecology is specifically adapted to, and dependent upon, the inundated floodplain conditions occuring with the annual rains. The absence of floodplain extension and adequate fish populations alone puts at risk an entire community of tree species dependent on the fish's yearly feeding and seed dispersal habits, as discussed in Chapter 2.

This is only one example of numerous and complex relationships which support the entire ecosystem. The absence of the annual fertile deposits of upriver silts is another singular impact which threatens the survival of a habitat adapted to annual nutrient replenishment.

Economic criticisms plague the Balbina project. Its poor efficiency and planning in comparision with other hydroelectric schemes of a similar scale, and the high cost of its construction, have led to strong denunciations by economists as well as ecologists. So far the construction costs have reached $700 million. Each kilowatt of electricity to be produced has cost more than $3,000 (*O Estado de São Paulo* 1988) while other hydroelectric dams produce energy at a much cheaper rate: a project on the São Francisco River has cost $600/KW, while the Itumbiara project cost only $370/KW. In addition to the already exorbitant construction costs, the Balbina dam is not expected to be useful or necessary for more than a few years. "In reality Eletronorte spent a fortune on a project that in 1996 will be totally unnecessary, when the Hydroelectric Dam of Cachoeira Porteira enters into operation" (*A Critica* 1988). Cachoeira Porteira is the dam planned to make up for Balbina's inability to supply the current demands of Manaus.

The economic demands of putting Balbina into operation have become even worse. When I visited Balbina in June 1988, generation of hydro-power was scheduled to begin in October of the same year (Santos 1988). The Manaus newspaper, *A Critica*, announced on 28 July that the opening of the dam was delayed, but confirmed that it was to be operational by February 1989. Just three days later it was revealed that the dam could not be put into operation at all – a "technical error" in planning for the reservoir had resulted in the lack of sufficient water pressure to turn the turbines required for the generation of electricity (*O Estado de São Paulo* 1988). Eletronorte has proposed the diversion of a neighbouring river to increase the size and force of the reservoir. The diversion would require the construction of a canal, through one of the few remaining areas of unaffected Waimiri-Atroari territory. The cost is projected at an additional $700 million, doubling the already exorbitant cost of the project.

The varied and extensive ramifications of the Balbina Dam have earned it the criticism and resentment of many sectors affected or concerned by the impacts of its construction. Resistance to further development in the region and to grand-scale hydroelectric development in general has grown as a result. In addition, efforts to rehabilitate the affected people and ecosystems are receiving much attention. The forms of opposition, and demands for reform or compensation, which have resulted from the experience of the Balbina hydroelectric project are of importance when looking ahead to similar projects planned for the future of Amazonia.

Resistance

In the area of Balbina, the experience of the Waimiri-Atroari spurred involvement by the Catholic Indian Missionary Council (CIMI) and resulted in the creation of the Movement to Support the Waimiri-Atroari Resistance (MAREWA). One of the main players in both of these organizations has been Egydio Schwade, founder of MAREWA. Before settling in the town of Presidente Figueredo and establishing MAREWA, Schwade lived in the Waimiri-Atroari Reserve under the auspices of CIMI. He conducted a literacy education programme in order to teach the Waimiri-Atroari to use their language in written communication.

The indigenous people perpetuate records of their history and knowledge through verbal traditions, rather than written language. The process Schwade taught is termed *alphabetização*, based on the teachings of Paulo Friere. For many years, Friere's methods of teaching were considered radically subversive, and he had been jailed and deported by the military government during its rule. When he was allowed to return, the successes of his literacy programmes were so impressive that in 1989 he was appointed Sao Paulo's Minister of Education.

Alphabetização is taught using associations between cultural experiences or sounds and written symbols in the national language. The resulting literacy would enable communication between the Waimiri-Atroari and the national society. Many cultural symbols and experiences of the Waimiri-Atroari were revealed through Schwade's process. Sounds were associated with animals from their natural surroundings, and words were given historical significance. At his home, Schwade showed me drawings by some of his students, which went so far as to relate the presence of Brazilian armies in their villages. Doroty and Egydio Schwade had been expelled from the Waimiri-Atroari Reserve by the government, for involvement in "subversive activities". They resettled in Presidente Figueredo, the town closest to both the reserve and Balbina, where they founded MAREWA (Schwade 1988).

MAREWA's main activities in resistance to the process of extinction being suffered by the Indian people is the recording of the history of the Waimiri-Atroari, as recounted by them, especially in relation to regional developments such as Balbina. As all Indian lands are restricted government areas, it is often difficult to gain access, particularly in regions affected by development projects in progress.

It is rare for the internal histories of the peoples affected to reach a public forum, but CIMI distributes information published from MAREWA in Manaus, and current works are in progress for release abroad. The education of the public about the culture, traditional life, and effective genocide of the Waimiri-Atroari in the face of Brazil's development is the focus of MAREWA's work. The histories are intended to gain support for these and other Indian peoples in similar circumstances, as they struggle against projects imposed on their lands which result in cultural and physical deterioration, or the ultimate death of their people.

In the case of the rural farmers or riverine communities of the Brazilian society, opposition to the Balbina Dam has taken a more mainstream approach. Using the laws and structures established by the government, the Rural Agricultural Workers' Union (the *syndicato*) is working to attain a legal claim to the lands to which they have been relocated. However, Brazilian unions are themselves government-funded, with strict guidelines to monitor their registration and actions. Only one union for a particular labour group is permitted for each municipality. In the municipality of Presidente Figueredo, the concern of the acting union is to obtain legal titles for displaced farmers. However, a rival group of large landholders is attempting to replace the current union, and its goals.

More fundamental policy changes are being addressed by alternative political parties campaigning in Presidente Figueredo and throughout Brazil. Both the Workers' Party (Partido dos Trabalhadores) and the Brazilian Socialist Party (Partido Socialista Brasileiro) widely oppose Brazil's development policies as impositional, and campaign for more participatory development planning on a local level. While blocking the construction of Balbina is no longer possible, in other areas of Amazonia more timely participation and opposition to development plans is being initiated.

Attempts by environmental advocates or ecologists in Brazil to ameliorate the effects of hydroelectric construction, or to prevent the initiation of projects, commonly stem from the scientific community or the educated middle class. More removed from the realities of immediate human impacts, environmental advocacy focuses largely on the conservation of ecosystems and the protection of fauna and flora. Yet, far from being a concern of privilege, environmental protection is seen as being necessary to the condition and quality of life. In locally-based conservation arguments, the impacts of the historical use and abuse of Amazonia's resources and lands form the basis for advocating present and future conservation measures. Economic as well as social dependency on the Amazonian environment tie all people more closely to the land than is common in the developed nations.

The understanding that unpredictable and uncontrollable repercussions often result from poorly planned development, and of how these effects have led to resource depletion and decline in the quality of life, form the core of the environmental movement that is only now developing a widespread base in Amazonia.

Most activity in environmental advocacy is channelled through the universities, the press and sympathetic government agencies. The University of Amazonas has sponsored open debates on the Balbina Dam. In August 1987, the purpose of one such debate was to reach conclusions on the practicality and desirability of implementing similar projects in the future. Acting as a public forum of information on the dam, and a strategic means of influencing policy through the inclusion of various government officials, the debate reached some very definitive conclusions. One participant summarized: "Development is not just if it does not consider the worker, the majority, the Indian, and the environment" (*A Critica* 1987). The Brazilian press has long followed the progress of Balbina, and in July 1987 headlined the denunciation by the director of SEMA, the Special Secretary for the Environment: "Balbina never again! This is the most stupid [project] of the Brazilian energy programme. It is an absurdity. It is unjustifiable. It has to be the last. Brazil cannot afford to repeat disasters like this" (Jordan 1987). A year later, when it was discovered that the dam would not function at all as constructed, *The State of São Paulo* carried the headline "The Scandal of the Balbina Hydroelectric Dam", and strongly denounced the planning for the project, and the incapabilities and mismanagement of Eletronorte (*O Estado de São Paulo* 1988).

Environmental impact statements and research conducted during and after construction to detail the ecological effects of large-dam construction are carried out by the National Institute for Amazon Research (INPA). INPA is the government agency through which all research in Amazonia must be channelled. The relative size of the staff in comparison with the research needed, and the speed of development and forest destruction, accounts in part for the Institute's lack of knowledge about the Amazonian ecosystems and the effects of large dams in particular. The scientists who work for INPA are drawn from both Brazilian and international communities.

Since the initiation of Balbina, several employees of INPA have been especially critical and outspoken with respect to the dam. Ecologist Phillip Fearnside has said: "The construction of the Balbina Hydroelectric Dam was a great mistake and will be even worse if they continue construction after it was proved that good conditions for efficiency do not exist" (*A Critica* 1988). In his office on the outskirts of Manaus, Fearnside explained to me that definitive research documenting the negative ecological effects which follow the completion of hydroelectric dams are often not released or even finished due to a cut or suspension of funds before the final stages of the research can be completed. Frequently the findings are never reported, resulting in an insufficient database for determining the ecological consequences of the dams.

On the surface it would appear that all sectors of Brazil's society concerned about large-scale hydroelectric development are involved in their own manner of promoting policy reform in relation to the environment and the people affected. However, the efficacy of these efforts is greatly reduced by the manner in which various groups approach the problem. Central to this is the insulation and fractionalization of the concerned sectors in relation to one another: the strengthening and expansion of these non-governmental organizations is sorely needed. It is extremely difficult for Amazonians to invest significant time and money when their primary and constant concern is simply maintaining a subsistence-level income or crop production for their families.

The lack of non-governmental assistance in Amazonia impairs the ability of the people to organize effective resistance. Yet, the lessons learned at Balbina have offered significant directions for the future of conservation and human-rights struggles. Progress in alternative forms of opposition and reform is strengthening the resistance to new development plans now being revealed for Amazonia.

5. ALTAMIRA–XINGU: BIRTH OF THE RESISTANCE

I came to the town of Altamira by way of the Transamazon Highway, in a *leito*, or night bus. The Transamazon was intended to open the Amazon to easy access and development, but remains a dirt road gouged with ditches and overgrown in the areas which have not already been cleared for plantations or ranches. The 18-hour trip from Santarem began in daylight, but there was no fascinating forest life to watch as we entered the interior. The forest had been cleared for miles on either side of the road. Occasionally, a house or group of cattle indicated a human presence, but most of the land appeared abandoned. Many of the migrants who settled here in the 1970s have moved on to new farms, or to look for work in the cities. It was not until hours later, when the bus was dark and we were all sleeping, that we entered the rainforest.

I was woken by branches and leaves smacking against the bus, as we pressed through sections of road barely visible through the foliage. The growth of the forest constantly reclaims the road, and only persistent maintenance keeps it passable. Looking out of the window, I peered straight into the darkness under the tree canopy, and imagined all the night creatures running for cover. We were travelling in good weather, but during the rains the buses must travel in pairs, in order to draw each other out of the mud. In the driest seasons, a single truck will raise clouds of red dust, choking the air for miles behind. Travelling under relatively good conditions we arrived in Altamira only a couple of hours behind schedule. This is where the newest series of dams, the Xingu Hydroelectrics Complex, is scheduled for construction.

The Xingu Complex is one of the largest of Brazil's projects for energy production outlined in the 2010 Plan. The proposed sites span the length of the Xingu River basin through which flows one of the major tributaries to the main trunk of the Amazon. Located in the eastern Amazonian state of Para, the Xingu basin represents one of the most undeveloped regions in all of Brazil. The hydroelectric complex would implant six major dams along its rivers and create the largest reservoir in the world.

The initiation site for the complex is the town of Altamira, where the Transamazon Highway crosses the Xingu River. In the initial plans for economic integration of the northern regions Altamira was an original "development pole" of Amazonia. Business and human infrastructures were to have been established sufficiently to facilitate intensive regional development.

By 1988, the official population of Altamira had reached 38,000 (Eletronorte/CNEC 1988a), a mixed population of government employees, businessmen, gold miners and labourers. An extensive shanty town had sprung up along the waterways, occupied largely by families whose land had failed in the colonization programmes and recent migrants to town looking for jobs in the construction of the dams. Unlike most Amazonian towns transportation to and from Altamira by river is limited, and most travel and commerce depends on the road conditions. Downstream from the town lies a series of unnavigable waterfalls; upstream is Indian land rarely visited by Brazilians.

The first of the Xingu Dams, the Kararão, is scheduled to be built on the falls just downstream from Altamira (see Figure 5.1). Projected to flood an area of 1,225 km², the reservoir will inundate part of the town of Altamira, a portion of the Transamazon Highway, tracts of rainforest and Indian lands. The projected firm energy produced will be 4,675 MW (Eletronorte 1988). Operating at full

Figure 5.1: Dams of the Altimira–Xingu Complex (Xingu basin indigenous lands)

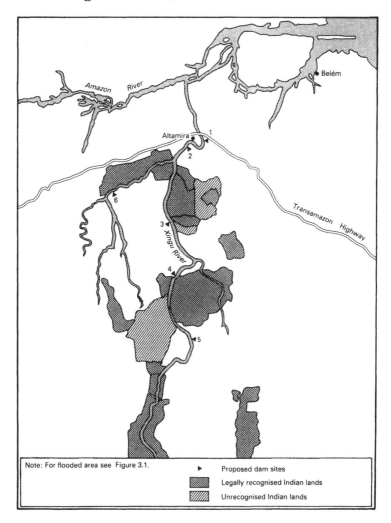

Note: For flooded area see Figure 3.1.
Source: CPI 1988; Prelazia do Xingu

capacity and in conjunction with the complementary effects of future dams, Kararão will have a potential of 11,000 MW when the complex is finished. Total generation potential for the entire project of six units is foreseen at 20,400 MW (Viveras de Castro and Andrade 1988). Today, Altamira requires only 40–50 MW for itself. The demand for energy from the Xingu Complex will come from the urban/industrial centres of the northeastern and southern states. Kararao is scheduled to supply electricity to the city of São Paulo, necessitating the extension of transmission lines 2,600 km to the south.

Kararao is included in Eletronorte's plans for initiating construction over the next five years and a general "power sector loan" has been requested from the World Bank to assist in Brazil's energy-development programme during this time. As a result of concern over its negative environmental and social impacts, the second of the dams, Babaquara, has been dropped from the list of projects to be undertaken during this period. However, many issues still remain unsettled about the effects of Kararao. Brazil has been unwilling to reconsider the plans for its construction, although the concerns of the people and regions to be affected have not been satisfied. Opposition is growing and, in an unprecedented movement, local concerns are uniting in a precautionary resistance.

The Kararão hydroelectric scheme

Inventories for the hydroelectric potential of the Xingu River basin were conducted between 1975 and 1980. Six sites were chosen for maximum generating potential from the water resources of the region. The resultant plan of hydroelectric development along the rivers comprise the Xingu Hydroelectric Complex. Five dams along the Xingu River and one on the Iriri are outlined in the plan. The combination of the first two, Kararão and Babaquara, would concentrate 70% of the energy to be generated in the complex. At one time referred to as the Altamira Complex, these two dams have now been separated due to serious problems associated with the plans for Babaquara. Babaquara has been delayed, pending re-evaluation, and will probably require some changes if international financial assistance is to be sought for its construction. Kararao is expected to be ready for operation in 1999.

One of the major justifications for the construction of Kararao is the "cheap" energy it will produce, which would decrease Brazil's dependency on foreign oil. The firm energy projected is 4,675 MW, estimated as the equivalent of 23,000 barrels of oil (Eletronorte/CNEC 1988b). The power sector has calculated that the savings in oil consumption will amount to $4.6 million/day, or $1.7 billion/year. However, for the first five years Kararao will only be operating at an average of 2,200 MW, translating to less than half the savings projected, or approximately $800 million/yr. Compared with the costs of constructing the hydroelectric dam, the savings begin to dwindle. The cost of construction is estimated at $5.8 billion. If no costs beyond strict construction are considered, and the dam operates as planned, it would take over six years in operation to begin to realize some of the savings in oil imports. Additionally, Eletronorte's figures do not account for maintenance or operation costs. The cost of the hydroelectric project rises again when interest rates on the money borrowed for construction are taken into account. It is difficult to determine whether the financial argument holds significant weight, especially against the additional costs of the human and environmental rehabilitation which would be required. However, Eletronorte claims that the "low" cost of construction will permit investment in extensive transmission lines to transport the electricity to the centres of market demand in the rest of the country, and still offer competitive prices. Kararão will supply the growing industries of São Paulo.

Eletronorte has taken policy steps to alleviate the negative impacts of its development programmes, but written policy often delivers no protection or compensation where it is necessary. The World Bank has been instrumental in the drawing up of an "Environmental Master Plan" for Brazil, outlining the guidelines for environmental and human protection measures in the projects for which funding is requested. However, the Bank admits that Brazil has failed to meet these guidelines after loans have been granted in the past. In the case of Kararão, the viability and impact studies had all been drafted by 1988. The local response shows little confidence in the willingness or ability of the responsible agencies to take sufficient measures to alleviate the impacts on the local peoples.

The area of influence of the Kararao Dam includes the lands to be directly flooded and those regions indirectly affected by the project's implementation. The construction of roads and transmission lines, and any area whose subsistence or commercial activities are altered by the dam's construction, are included in the areas indirectly affected. The regions which will suffer the most direct impact from the project are those along the road and river routes from Altamira to the nearby town of Vitoria, and along the 100 km of the Transamazon highway between Altamira and Belo Monte, including all the communities previously settled there by the government's colonization projects. Finally, two Indian villages a short distance upstream from Altamira will be lost to the floodwaters.

The town of Vitoria is a short distance from Altamira by road. It is a small commerce and transport centre on the downstream side of the waterfalls, providing the only river route that connects Altamira to the urban centre of Belem at the Amazon delta. Much more reliable and less time-consuming than the roads, this route facilitates a stable exchange of market goods between Altamira and the city. With the dam affecting river flows, the future of transport and commerce between Altamira and Belem is threatened. Vitoria and locations downstream will no longer be able to use the river for subsistence or transportation, suffering the same effects as the communities downstream from the

Balbina dam. In this case, though, a much greater population will be affected, taking into account the population of Altamira which depends heavily on goods coming into Vitoria and marketing its own produce by the same route.

I toured Vitoria and the route downstream by boat. Leaving Altamira, it is 45 minutes to Vitoria by road, circumventing the waterfalls which cannot be navigated. In Vitoria I discovered it would be three days until the next boat would leave for Belem, my final destination. Deciding not to return to Altamira, I went to find a hotel. The town was one mile long by half-a-mile wide, and had no hotel. Fortunately there was a small store and a *launch*, the common bar/restaurant which shades and quenches the thirst of all Amazonian townspeople during the midday sun. Assured that I could get food, I asked the boat owner if I could sleep on board. I strung my hammock between two rails and made myself comfortable.

The bustle of the boats on the beach was constant, transporting and unloading shipments between Altamira and the city. The town's life depended upon the river. On the third day of waiting, more hammocks were strung up on board and the boat was transformed into a medley of colours and smells which would accompany us to Belem. We left at sunset. The first two days of travel took us down the Xingu, to its confluence with the Amazon. Small settlements, isolated huts with agricultural gardens, and a steady stream of commercial riverboats filled the scene at every gap in the forest. The communities here, and their stream of goods into Altamira, would all be disrupted with the construction of the dam.

Upstream from Kararão the impacts will be much more direct. All lands in the flood area below 96 metres (264 feet) above sea level will be inundated (Santos and Andrade 1988). Eletronorte will be responsible for the relocation and compensation of the displaced rural and urban Brazilian families, and relocation plans for the indigenous peoples affected will be the responsibility of FUNAI. Many of the people in the rural areas affected had been settled on their lands by the government's colonization programmes of the 1970s. These families live along the stretch of the Transamazon Highway which will be flooded by the reservoir. The highway will have to be rerouted and the families relocated. People of the rural riverine communites will be displaced as well. It will be more difficult to transfer these families to comparable areas and they are likely to have to adjust to a new manner of subsistence along the banks of the lake, or away from any water source if the usual problems of disease vectors and transmission are introduced to the region. In total, 328 rural families will be displaced by the dam's reservoir (IDESP Files; Brock 1988).

In Altamira, a large section of the town itself will be flooded. Here, another 7,090 people will be affected and displaced, constituting almost 20% of Altamira's population. The town will have to be greatly expanded to accommodate new homes for these families alone. Many have no legal claims to their land or homes and will not be compensated. Additionally, a population boom is expected with new employees entering Altamira in connection with the dams. A "residential village" of 7,200 homes will be built for the new workers. It is expected that the construction will employ 12,500 people directly, and involve a total of 30,000 when including infrastructure employment and markets generated by the activity of the project.

Kararao, being only the first of the Xingu Complex dams and closest to the urban centres, will have the least impact on the indigenous communities of the Xingu. In all, Chief Paiakan Kaiapo, of the Indian village of Aukre, estimates that 35,000 Indian people will be affected by the complex as a whole (International Rivers Network 1989). The first dam at Kararão will displace two Indian villages which are regularly involved in trade with Altamira: Jurua and Trincheiro, which are home to 78 Brazilian Indians (Brock 1988). The plans for their relocation have not yet been released. Generally, FUNAI establishes Indian posts, settles the displaced native peoples in a government-regulated community, and works to integrate them into the national society, as has been dictated by the Constitution (Amnesty International 1988b).[1] Indirectly, through infrastructure and colonization increases, peoples of the Arara, Kararao, Kotirero, Ipixuna, Bacaja, Porokone, Apetewa and Cururua villages will also be affected by the Kararão Dam.

Eletronorte's environmental feasibility studies of 1985–6 identify that approximately 10%, or 612 hectares, of the indigenous territory of Paquicamba will be flooded. Many of these peoples have spoken out against the dam. The opposition of the Indian peoples is the most active public protest against dam construction that has yet emerged.

Eletronorte recognizes that the entire area to be affected by the dams is a "frontier area, in the process of occupation and transformation" (Eletronorte 1988). It intends to bring local benefits to and generate new businesses in the region, "principally during the term of the works" (Eletronorte/CNEC 1988a). Yet Eletronorte recognizes that the land as it is, prior to transformation by development, is of value as well. The preliminary environmental impact statement describes the forest region to be flooded as: "unexplored forests, still little known, an abundant fauna in unaltered habitats, unpolluted rivers, and unexplored mineral riches" (Eletronorte 1988). It is unlikely that much of this will be salvaged, with the exception of the minerals already being exploited by individual gampineiros. Perhaps the most significant point to be made about the regional impacts is that the studies of Eletronorte provide evidence that the agency is aware of the level of disruption likely to be created by the dams, yet plans to proceed with implementation. The environmental-impact statement claims that the viability of the project was determined by a comparison between the negative impacts (costs) of construction and the benefits of development, on local, regional and national scales. The reaction of the local people to Eletronorte's interpretation of this cost-benefit analysis suggests that the national benefits of construction, in the analysis of Eletrobras, hold priority over all local considerations. In short, the Kararão Dam and the Xingu Hydroelectric Complex represent the colonization of Amazonia and the extraction of its energy resources, much as earlier experiences witnessed the exploitation of the Amazon's land, natural (physical) resources, and human labour.

Resistance

The forces organizing opposition to the dams of the Xingu Complex generally stem from three sectors of society, as outlined in the Introduction. The ecologists and environmentalists, primarily concerned with the state of the forest and natural resources, are mostly trained scientists and the educated middle class. The people working for social justice or political reform are concerned mainly with imbalances in wealth and power in Brazil, and the usurpation of the poor by the élite. Their specific concern with respect to the dams is the marginalization of the Amazonian Brazilians for the advancement of the "nation". The Amazonian Brazilians are generally poor rural or displaced urban wellers, and labourers. Finally, the indigenous peoples and their activist supporters are concerned with the physical and cultural survival of Amazonia's native peoples. Historically, the Indians themselves have not acted as a political force in Brazil, and live independently from the state until "contact", at which point they are drawn into society at its lowest level. Their supporters tend to be middle- or upper-class liberals, and the international activist community.

Many of the distinctions between these groups begin to break down when all sectors are affected by a development project with widespread impacts. Yet the lines remain drawn, often stifling the effectiveness of the resistance. In the past, opposition to a particular project or plan for development has not emerged until after the effects become visible, which is of course after the project has been initiated or even completed.

Recently, some of these barriers to effective opposition have begun to be overcome. The reaction thus far to the announcement of plans for the Xingu Complex has revealed a powerful political force emerging from the unification of the affected peoples. In many ways, Kararao has become the embodiment of Brazil's history of disruptive development, and not without significant realism or reason.

Environmentalists/ecologists

Responses to the plans for hydroelectric development along the Xingu river have been represented by scattered opposition from biologists and ecologists who have worked in the region. While often preferring to stay out of the political realm, scientists have conducted surveys of the region to be flooded and the potential effects have identified quite a few major problems. In the environmental-impact statement (RIMA), scientists point to the intensification of erosion processes as a likely consequence of the construction of the dam. The inundation of natural forest leading to the loss of valuable plant and animal species is pinpointed, as well as the additional disruption resulting from the loss of habitat and migration paths. Changes in water quality and especially in health conditions due to the introduction of diseases such as malaria, yellow fever, hepatitis and leishmaniasis are all problems researchers have attempted to bring to the fore. The RIMA gives only cursory attention to these problems, identifying what will result from construction on a physical level, but failing to extrapolate to the biotic and social consequences. The anticipated potential impacts are presented only in list form, with little further discussion of the implications. All research must proceed under the government agencies. To step beyond the bounds of proper process almost certainly results in dismissal. The confines presented by government employment typically hinder the ability for participation in a more progressive conservationist movement.

Non-governmental organizations (NGOs) and the press both play a much more dynamic role in promoting environmental protection in Amazonia. Yet, unlike effective work from the "inside", they may not be able to affect policy as directly as strong recommendations issued in a RIMA. However, in relation to popular opinion, the press is arguably the most effective voice for environmental ethics. Referring to changes since the restoration of democracy in 1985, it is reported that: "With press freedom restored, newspapers have taken to exposing official violence, corruption, nepotism, environmental abuse and social injustice, obliging Brazilians to see their own country in a new, crudely realistic light" (*New York Times* 1989b). While it is virtually impossible to secure information from the government about development plans in progress, the press will often release strong criticisms against impacts or inefficiencies as they are discovered. When the failure of Balbina was revealed, the São Paulo newspapers headlined the "scandal", and gave due attention to the environmental atrocities of the project. Eletronorte recently opened a Public Relations Department in an attempt to improve the media image of the agency and its projects.

The role of NGOs in promoting environmental reforms is limited, as are all NGO activities in Amazonia, but they are probably the strongest organizations in the stance they take. One organization which has survived 20 years celebrated its anniversary in 1988. SOPREN, the Society for the Preservation of Natural and Cultural Resources of Amazonia, recognizes its continued slow struggle in the advertisement marking its second decade – "20 years of putting a stop to the destruction of Amazonia ... we do not have much to commemorate." The founder of SOPREN, Camil Viana, still campaigns rigorously against environmentally destructive projects and attempts to educate all who will listen. In an interview at his home in Belem, Viana summed up his perspective on the Xingu Complex:

These projects have been characterized by a brutal aggression
to the environment. . . . And what's more curious, impoverishment of the region. . . . We have severe problems from
the Tucurui Dam to here. New diseases are appearing, the
fish have vermin, the waters of the river changed colour,
the margins of the lake and the islands are being destroyed.
Briefly, it seems that we are living in a situation of chaos
. . . what we are going to flood [on the Xingu] in minerals, in
uncultivated land, in species of flora and fauna which could be
used to heal diseases, I don't know. . . . I, today, at one in the
morning, said I was going to fight against injustice. . . . This is
a suicide operation.

(Viana 1988)

Finally, SOPREN has been able· to initiate a list of
programmes in education, research and consultation. It has
succeeded in being one stronghold of information and support
outside the often immobilized government agencies.

Central to the shortcomings of the environmental
movement in Amazonia is the tendency for many of the
people involved, particularly academics and scientists, to
avoid the political arena. Many of the people who have
the knowledge necessary to affect policy, in terms of
research data or the perspective of historical analysis,
are not themselves affected enough to engage in issues
of political conflict. As in the United States, concerns
for the environment are often considered the "luxury"
of mainstream society and the upper classes. While the
environment is in fact a concern of the lower classes, who
require its health for their own survival, the connections
often fail to be made across wide class and cultural barriers.
Historically, these divisions have detracted from the success
of conservation efforts. While recent attempts to examine
the roots of environmental issues have begun to recognize
and overcome these barriers, the divisions still continue to
weaken overall goals for environmental protection.

Social justice/minority political parties

The concerns of popular social-justice movements and affiliated political parties lie primarily with the position of the rural poor in Brazil's political-economic class structure. Rarely is the position of the Indians, at an even lower level within the class structure, considered as a part of these struggles. The means of opposition open to the rural poor to work on these issues are primarily through populist organization, labour unions and political representation within the party structure.

Efforts towards securing land titles below Balbina are being negotiated by the labour union there, and in Altamira the same union, the Rural Agricultural Workers' *Syndicato*, is preparing in advance for the coming threat of the dams. Expecting massive relocations and loss of farmlands to the reservoir, the union is emerging in opposition to the dam, and preparing for land and compensation negotiations before people are displaced. However, apart from being a lobbying force, the unions are not involved in the decision-making process. Here, local political parties opposed to the construction of Kararao have taken a stand.

The Brazilian Socialist Party (PSB) and the Workers' Party (PT) are the two most successful alternative political parties in Amazonia. Throughout the region they are campaigning for the local people and in opposition to the national development policies. The post of Deputy in Altamira was held by the PSB in 1988. In July, it was campaigning for the office of Prefeito (closely analagous to mayor) of Altamira on a platform of opposition to Eletronorte's dams programme. I attended one lively rally held in a centrally located park one night after dark. The makeshift stagelights and crowds of people and children created such a vibrancy that, on hearing cheers of support for the denunciations made against Eletronorte, one could imagine it as a scene from a revolution. The determination of the working-class settlers who spoke out clearly held hope for a new Amazonia. The PT holds the same position towards the dams and this platform has received widespread support. Some attempts have been made at alliances between the two parties, but as of July 1988, these had been unsuccessful (Correa and Andrade 1988). Such divisions between groups with compatible interests are characteristic of the types of rifts which frustrate the goals of the social-change movement in Amazonia.

The implementation of the *grandes projectos* is only one area in which the rural peasant parties differ from national politics. With the increase in strength of state and local governments, regional positions and decisions on development policies may begin to have greater influence. The ability of colonialist projects to be implemented in resistant areas will be made more difficult if the opposition works not only within the law, but *is* the law in affected areas. With the new Constitution and democratic governance, there is great opportunity for the advancement of local-level decision making. While it is impossible to tell at this early stage, the prospects for the continued involvement of regional parties holds much hope for long-suppressed Amazonians. It is expected that more confidence and participation in a democratic, partisan government will further strengthen their abilities for local self-determination.

The most obvious of the shortcomings associated with the Brazilian social justice movement is the apparent or actual exclusion of the Indian peoples. Concerns for social and political equality are often not extended to the indigenous people, even by people fighting for the same rights for themselves. The words of one Eletronorte social worker with respect to the Movement to Support the Waimiri-Atroari Resistance are typical of this attitude. Referring to MAREWA's founder, he said, "Egydio is a European who came to work with the Indians; these people are Brazilians who came to survive for themselves" (Lange 1988). Egydio Schwade, though of German descent, was in fact born and raised in Brazil, yet a means had to be found by which to dismiss the value of his work.

Clashes between the Brazilian peasants and Indian people have long been a part of the frontier experience. Unfortunately, this rivalry has blinded many in both groups to the larger inequalities of the government's programmes. Both Brazilian peasants and Brazilian Indians are used by the government interests in the process of opening the Amazon to large-scale development.

A common example of this process is demonstrated by the federally sponsored colonization programmes. The colonization of displaced or urban escapee peasants on Amazonian lands serves dual purposes for the government's long-term business interests. As was the case in the Plan for National Integration (PIN), the settlement of peoples on free land, with the condition that they clear and "improve" it, paves the way for larger landholders and business to move in at a later stage. Less work is then required to establish forms of land use such as cattle ranching, agricultural mass production, or plantation farming. The bulk of the work has been done by the peasant. Second, the colonization of an area by an influx of Brazilian peasants in need of land solves a great part of the Indian problem. Those who have not already been struck by disease will often fall in direct conflict with the peasants claiming their lands. The importance of recognizing the history of this second problem, the government's pitting of peasant against Indian as a means to its own end, is crucial to the mending of the gaps between these two sectors of society. An alliance between the Brazilian peasants and Indian peoples affected by the government's plans for hydroelectric development has the potential for unparalleled success as a resistance force.

The initiation of such alliances has been attempted recently by the rubber tappers of Acre and the local indigenous communities. The "Amazon Alliance" proposed connecting areas of "extractive reserves" from which the tappers could collect rubber from protected forest areas, and Indian reserves situated in the centre of the tappers' lands, which would be provided with a "buffer zone". The plan was applauded internationally, and an award given to Chico Mendes, its creator, by the United Nations Environment Programme (UNEP). Mendes's efforts to protect the forests and peoples of Acre eventually cost him his life. Chico Mendes Filho was assassinated in December 1988. Two cattle ranchers (a father and son) have been implicated in his murder but no trial has been held. Despite this, initiatives with the unity of Mendes's plan continue to be sought, in an effort to meet the basic needs of peasants and Indians throughout Amazonia.

Native peoples/human rights activists

The indigenous rights movement in Brazil has achieved the greatest level of integration among the issues that have been discussed. To a greater extent than environmentalists or social justice parties, the indigenous peoples of Amazonia and their supporters have recognized the links between themselves, their forests, and the national society in which they now live. Historically, Indian resistance to colonization and development had been demonstrated through warfare between Indians and the intruders on their lands. This held true when conflicts broke out with the earliest explorers, and is still true today in connection with people entering Amazonia on the heels of government projects. Recently, however, Amazonia's indigenous peoples have been learning new ways in which to oppose and fight against the encroachment and degradation of their lands. While in many ways the new Indian resistance may appear to have come too late, it is becoming the hope of the peoples who remain, who are committed to their lands, and who want to remain "Indian".

Since 1967, FUNAI has been the only avenue through which the Indian peoples of Brazil could legitimately negotiate for their rights. The legal structure of the government of Brazil made the Indian peoples wards of the state and FUNAI was the agency assigned to look after their welfare. The corruption and abuses of FUNAI in this capacity have been referred to in previous chapters. The difficulties the Indian peoples have met in claiming their rights through FUNAI have led to NGOs attempting to expose the abuses and oppose government involvement in developing indigenous lands. MAREWA is an example of this form of resistance. Schwade's purpose in founding MAREWA was to educate the public about the history of the Waimiri-Atroari with respect to the onslaught of industry and development on their lands. Many early organizations took this route where possible, aiming to speak for the Indians where they could not speak for themselves.

In Yanomami territory a similar group began to collect information and expose the fate of the peoples there, as well as their lack of government protection. Both Claudia Anjudar, founder of the Committee for the Creation of the Yanomami Park (CCPY), and Schwade of MAREWA, were expelled from Indian lands where they were respectively engaged in medical and educational work. Following their expulsion, each set up a non-governmental support and information network to strengthen the voice of the Indian peoples, having recognized the government's failure, to meet their basic needs and rights. The attention of the international community was focused on Brazil during this time, and alliances began to form to support the work of Indian rights activists within the country.

My introduction to Claudia Anjudar took place in her living room, which I mistakenly walked into assuming the address I had for CCPY was an office, rather than a private residence. Despite the intrusion, she welcomed me and began to explain her work. The government plans to isolate Yanomami communities in small, widely separated Indian parks. The rest of the region throughout which they are dispersed will serve as sites for intensive development, particularly mining and military installations. The fragmentation of the Yanomami serves as a flagrant example of disrespect for their culture and the wish to keep them from developing political unity. CCPY has been working for ten years to establish a continuous reserve for the Yanomami on their traditional lands.

In many cases the rural poor, labour unions and environmentalists have not recognized their affinity with the Indian rights issues. However, new innovations for extending the voice of the Indian peoples have begun to manifest themselves throughout Amazonia. In Altamira, a group of journalists found a novel means towards correcting this gap. As recently as 1987, the greater Altamira region did not have a local newspaper. Neither relevant political news nor local events had an outlet for dissemination to the community, and the state and city papers printed news and views irrelevant to the people of the rural areas.

In April 1987 the first local newspaper began publication. *O Kaiapó*, named for the regional Indian group, became the source of news and information for the rural region. The editor and journalists were publishing for a political agenda very different from the federal and urban interests, thus opening an avenue of information and inquiry on plans affecting the local people and the indigenous communities with whom they share the Xingu basin. Invasion of lands, rela tionships with the Indians, and plans for the hydroelectric complex were made the subject of public knowledge and opinion. Suzanna Correa, a journalist for the paper, described the publication as "an instrument of the Indian peoples, so they would have a forum to verse their complaints or ideas" to the wider public (Correa 1988).

The publication of *O Kaiapó* is a single example of the widespread connection the Indian movement in Brazil is making between its own goals, and the demand for conservation and social reform of Amazonia. However, the need for financial support for such projects limits their activities. The need for steady income in so economically depressed a region makes a strong commitment to social action without compensation especially difficult. In July 1988, Correa told me *O Kaiapó* was on the verge of folding.

Other means of informing people of the current dangers faced by Amazonia's indigenous peoples have proceeded more securely with financial support from the South or from outside Brazil. The Pro-Indian Commission (CPI), based in São Paulo, carried out an extensive study of the effects and undocumented impacts to be generated by the Kararaõ Dam. Much of the information on government projects is not made available to the public. Often, the local peoples to be affected by a project such as the Kararaõ Dam do not know in advance what the impact will be. This is especially true for the Indian peoples who are often not in contact with mainstream Brazilian society. CPI has completed a detailed dossier and critique of the Xingu Dams Complex entitled *Hydroelectrics of the Xingu: The State against the Indigenous People.*

The dossier includes information and data not previously released to the people affected, and is planned for distribution throughout the Altamira–Xingu region, with the assistance of the Indian Missionary Council (CIMI). Information to which the public has not had easy access, or which has been denied to local groups, will be openly distributed via the publication, "democratizing" access to information on the projects. This is part of the larger campaign to obtain public participation in decisions affecting the regional people, as well as linking the Indian and Brazilian struggles. *Hydroelectrics of the Xingu* includes a critical analysis of state manipulation of the rural and indigenous peoples, and even the concept of environment. The role of CPI in opposition to the Xingu Dams is to connect and expose the links between the Indians, the Brazilians and the environment, and to show how the government tries to hide these connections in its attempts to suppress the development of a unified resistance.

A great step was made in establishing the Indians themselves as a unified voice, apart from their government tutelage, with the creation of the Union of Indigenous Nations (UNI). After establishing its headquarters in São Paulo, UNI began to contact and unite Indian peoples from all over Brazil. UNI establishes an independent voice for the Indian people but is refused official recognition by the government. FUNAI is the only legally recognized organization of the indigenous peoples. Still, UNI has met with incomparable success in uniting Brazil's Indians and bringing their story and their demands to international attention.

A number of strong statements have been conveyed recently from Amazonia's Indian peoples to the Brazilian government. In 1988, Davi Yanomami received the UNEP Award for his work to protect the Yanomami Indians and their lands. In July 1988, 60 people from the Gaviao and Guajajara tribes in Imperatriz took over and occupied the regional FUNAI office to protest about the activities of a mining company on their lands (*O Liberal* 1988b).

Various means are being used by native peoples to claim their rights and to protest about the development plans of the national government which threaten their physical and cultural survival. The developing resistance to the Xingu Dams Complex is among the most successful of these demonstrations of the new Indian resistance. The Kayapo of the Xingu basin are leading this protest and have pulled together the support and co-operation of many diverse Indian groups throughout Amazonia, as well as members of the scientific, socio-political and activist communities in Brazil and abroad. They represent the progressive line in uniting the concerns of all the sectors affected by the government's large-scale development projects. Additionally, they have gone further than many politicians to learn just how to bring about change most effectively. As far as the Xingu Hydroelectric Complex is concerned, they appear to constitute the only resistance strong enough to be capable of stopping the building of the dams.

In January 1988, Chiefs Paiakan and Kube-i of the Kayapo received an invitation to attend a conference on the management of tropical rainforests in Miami, Florida. Recognition of their traditional forest-farming techniques came through the anthropologist Darrell Posey, who has studied with them for 12 years. The Kayapo accepted, and spoke during the conference about, news they had heard of a large dam to be constructed on their river, which would flood great portions of their land. Paiakan had already moved his people once as a result of the encroachment of miners on their tribal lands, and had decided that it was too late to continue moving away from development. They were looking for ways to stop the dam.

On the evening the Kayapo arrived in Miami, a film was shown to the conference audience. The film depicted the timely but arrogant observations of one anthropologist who lived with relatives of the Kayapo years before. Paiakan and Kube-i watched in silence, seeing again the death of friends and family they had already experienced first-hand. Following this, the Kayapo answered questions about European and American intrusions on their land, and the ways they sought to stop the coming phase of industrial development. It was an equally educational time for the Kayapo, as they finally learned of the specific plans for the dams. In Brazil, the government had neglected to inform them at all, let alone include them in consultations.

Several American environmental organizations invited the Kayapo to return to Washington, DC with them following the conference. The World Bank was in the process of considering a loan to Brazil's power sector which would support its hydroelectric energy development over the next five years. Meetings were arranged between the Kayapo and the World Bank, Congress and Treasury. Dr Posey accompanied the chiefs to act as translator. The Kayapo made their case to the financiers and revealed information about previous failures of the power sector to uphold World Bank policies with regard to the environment and indigenous peoples. Guarantees were reportedly secured that no financing would be approved to Brazil for further dam construction until all assurances for protection of the Kayapo and other peoples of the Xingu were obtained from the Brazilian government (*O Liberal* 1988a).

Upon their return to Brazil, the Kayapo and Dr Posey were repeatedly interrogated by the federal police, and in July 1988 Darrell Posey was charged with criminal interference in Brazil's internal affairs. The charges came under a foreigners' act prohibiting such activities by non-Brazilians (Law no. 6.815/80, Article 107). A month later the Kayapo chiefs were charged under the *same law*. International reaction to these measures rallied widespread support for the Kayapo and opposition to the Xingu Dams. The Kayapo continued to publicize their case and take advantage of opportunities for public action and denouncements. A number of events made this continued public resistance possible.

The three charged were all required to appear in court to make their statements. On the day Kube-i appeared, 200 Kayapo warriors danced in protest outside the courthouse. The judge assigned to hear Kube-i's statement refused to allow him to be heard in his traditional dress. Kube-i was ordered to return dressed "respectfully", in a formal shirt and trousers. The judge additionally ordered psychological tests for the Kayapo to determine their level of acculturation, or "Indianness". Finally, in February 1989, the cases against Posey, Paiakan and Kube-i were dropped in the appeal court. Counter-suits of discrimination for the judge's two orders are still pending. This occurred just before the Kayapo's next major protest was scheduled to begin.

The following week, beginning 21 February, in Altamira, the largest ever gathering of native Amazonians joined in protest against the Kararāo Dam. They began to organize a unified resistance of Indian peoples against development projects destructive to the peoples and environments of the Amazon. Led by the Kayapo, Indians from more than a dozen regions built a village on the site of the Kararāo Dam. If necessary, the Kayapo were prepared to take up permanent residence to stop the construction. Brazilian government officials and NGOs from around the world were present. By the end of the week, negotiations with Eletronorte were considered so successful that the occupation was ended. An Amazonian Indian movement had been established, and the Kayapo became a significant political influence in the plans for the Xingu Dams. During the course of that year, a resistance movement comprised of environmental and scientific interests, social justice parties, rural peasants, international supporters and Indian peoples had been founded. The groundwork for a unified Indian resistance within Amazonia has been laid, and the model of co-operation and recognition of compatible needs has been put forth for us by the people of the Kayapo.

The success of this movement probably lies with the action taken by the Kayapo shortly after their decision to oppose the processes of development. Paiakan explains that when they began to notice changes in the cycle of rains and the floods they took steps to find and oppose the forces causing the disruption:

> I remember when a different climate began to appear in the village. Some of the elders discussed this and decided that a very strong enemy was trying to change the life of the our tribe. . . . Now we understand that the enemy is the destruction of the habitat. They are changing our climate. They have changed the cycle of the rains. . . . So we went to the city and began to learn of what the white man is doing. . . . The young of the tribe must continue to live in the forest without losing control of it. They must secure and preserve the forest. . . . Because without the forest, how would we live?
>
> (Kaiapo 1988b)

The Kayapo divided their leadership. The traditional elders stayed in the villages to secure the continuation of traditions, the teaching of the children about the Kayapo way of life, and the survival of their culture. The younger, newly formed political leaders went to the cities to learn about Western culture, the government's development plans, and their intentions for the fate of the Indians. Through this, and through learning to use the modern tools which could help them, the Kayapo began to organize an effective resistance to the dams. They identified the people with similar concerns, adapted the use of video and tape equipment to their own purposes, and utilized the white's fascination with their culture to capture the attention of politicians and the media alike. Their successes in gaining their rights have extended even to influencing the drafting of the new Brazilian Constitution.

On the day when the indigenous rights clauses were being determined in the Constitution, several hundred Kayapo and other tribal leaders travelled to the Constituent Assembly to voice their demands in the drafting of their constitutional rights. This was the day I arrived in Brazil. Unable to contact any of the people I meant to talk with in Rio de Janeiro or São Paulo, I sat down to read the newspaper and discovered the reason. NGOs, government officials, Indian activists and over a hundred Indian representatives were seated in the Assembly drafting the new Indian rights bill. The organization for this appearance was co-ordinated by the UNI. The result has been the strongest Indian rights chapter ever to be written into Brazilian law. Foremost were two changes strengthening the abilities of the Indian peoples to defend themselves before the law. Previous laws defining any person who speaks Portuguese as no longer being Indian were revoked. Second, the Indian people were given the right to independent counsel in a court of law, where previously all legal dealings of the Indian people were conducted through FUNAI (CEDI 1989). In the case of the Xingu Dams protest this may have been a primary reason why the cases against Paiakan, Kube-i and Darrell Posey were eventually dropped.

The history of resistance to Brazil's development projects has been shown to be scattered and fragmented within its own forces. It has been easy to weaken populist resistance through the conditions of poverty which make independent social action difficult. The control of government agencies over almost all forms of inquiry or organization (such as government research agencies or labour unions) has placed limitations on the extent of information released or reforms people could attempt to introduce. The pitting of peasants against native peoples, and divisions between the élite and the poor, have been means by which the government disrupts the unification of opposition forces.

Recently, strides have been made in overcoming some of these barriers. The establishment of NGOs in Amazonia has given the people of the region more support in promoting reforms or opposing projects which threaten their means of survival. Most significantly, the overcoming of barriers between groups of people with compatible needs and goals has perhaps been the turning point in establishing an effective resistance to government development policies. The example of the Kayapo in particular has provided a model for meeting the needs for conservation and human rights in Amazonia.

Note

1. In the new Constitution a major victory was achieved by the Indian people on this point. Article 231 now states recognition of the Indian social organization and guarantees protection for their "physical and cultural reproduction". Previous Constitutions provided for their integration into the national society, rather than cultural protection (CEDI 1988; Santilli 1989). How relocation policy will change in response to the new Constitution remains undetermined.

6. UNDER THE POLITICS OF DEVELOPMENT

The validity of national Brazilian rhetoric in promoting its plans for hydroelectric development has been brought into question by the wide range of opposition to proposed projects. Specific goals of development – raising the standard of living, improving the quality of life or eliminating poverty in a developing region – are clearly denied to a great number of the people who are immediately affected by Brazil's energy-development plans. In fact, after evaluating the impacts of large-scale hydroelectric projects on local peoples, it is apparent that the benefits to industrialists and the central government élites, gained through increased energy production, are dependent upon the impoverishment and marginalization of Amazonia's poorer peoples. The strategies utilized by the Brazilian government to accomplish the transfer of resources from Amazonia to Brazil's power centres reveal their awareness of these effects. An understanding of the ideological roots of existing policy and the means used to realize its goals is important in formulating appropriate and effective strategies of resistance.

Forms of colonial domination are central to the power relationships which have permitted the realization of the *grandes projectos* in areas where there is resistance to their implantation. The "New Republic" of Brazil, in its recent return to institutional democracy, is less than five years old. The actualization of this democracy has met with varied degrees of success and participation from different parts of the country. In Amazonia, where basic infrastructures are still largely lacking, the more sophisticated forms of national institutions, such as legal and protective agencies, are often non-existent. The lack of these structures, or their domination and corruption by the persons in power, have stifled the region's ability to achieve the levels of participatory democracy which have emerged in other areas of Brazil. In Amazonia, the military retains official control of the northern perimeter, in a 150-km band around the border, in the interests of "national security" (*segurança nacional*). All political and developmental decisions to be made in this region fall under "Calha Norte", the Northern Trench plan, and are determined by the National Security Council. A full 14 per cent of the national territory falls under their jurisdiction (Hecht and Cockburn 1989). Air strips, army bases, mining, exploration, even the demarcation of Indian lands are taken out of the arena of public decisions, "excluding civil society, political parties and the legislature from debate on the issues" (Santilli 1989).

Throughout the rest of Amazonia, the long history of control by the politically and financially powerful, the military and the large landholders, has established a *modus operandi* which has been difficult to escape from without the democratic support and catalysts better established in the South, East and Centre-west of the country. Amazonian policy has always been, officially or unofficially, one of extracting resources from the region for profit elsewhere. The middlemen in these relationships have realized great profits and are not easily inclined to relinquish this power base to the new democracy. In order to maintain control in Amazonia, alliances have been made in many areas between the authorities and the financial élite. In this way the businesses implanted in Amazonia have enforced their "rights" to lands and maintained their control over local law. In many cases, large landholders will employ their own militia to ensure their authority. Local policy thus becomes one of serving the interests for extraction, export and profit elsewhere.

While Brazil strongly asserts its rights to developing Amazonia and defends its autonomy in formulating development policy in the region, this national level of decision-making recognizes its sizeable opposition within the nation as well as from other countries. The success of many other stages in initiating changes in Amazonia, under the label of development, have depended on a misrepresentation of Brazil's true intentions and policies. The first Plan for National Integration (PIN), the colonization of Amazonia as a form of social relief to give land to the landless, was later revealed to have been a tool to open the way to large businesses and landholdings. The second PIN withdrew titles to small landholdings and, instead, issued large plots to businesses which could more intensively develop Amazonia. Much of the work of initial clearing had already been accomplished. Large tracts had been cleared by the individuals whose land had failed.

A more transparent example is offered by the role of Brazil's first Indian agency. The Indian Protection Service (SPI) was created for the supposed purpose of mediating between the Indians and development, while insuring the integration of Amazonia. Publicly promoting the contact and pacification of the Amazonian Indians, the agency was eventually forced to disband with the release of reports about its bombing of the villages in its charge (Davis 1977). This incident and subsequent investigations exposed SPI as an agent of facilitation for government projects and as a contributor to the systematic extermination of the indigenous peoples. The rhetoric used to cover the agency's role further demonstrates Brazil's manner of shielding its "development" intents. Following this incident, the name of the agency was changed, but it is questionable that its policies have undergone an equal transformation.

The national government's intent to usurp one region or peoples for the benefit of another is often masked in rhetoric about public policies and agencies acting in the interests of the people. The facilitation of development goals by misrepresentation disperses opposition, as rhetoric and actual policy are confused. This diffuses opposition and reinforces the idea that Brazil speaks for a nation of peoples, when in fact there are many whom it does not represent. The national rhetoric is additionally aimed at the international lending institutions from whom Brazil receives financial assistance for its projects. Few sources would give money for the government élite's *true* goals, but "development" is a catchword that carries with it assumptions of a better standard of living.

The development of Amazonia has given us several examples of the actual results of such programmes. The experience to date with hydroelectric dams in the North has proved to be a continuation of the damages incurred by Amazonia for the benefit of an industrialized, élite Brazil. The assessment of previous plans has revealed the improportionate impacts suffered by the indigenous peoples. The extent to which in-digenous lands are targeted as development areas brings into suspicion the primary goals of Amazonian "development" projects. Again, considering the direct methods the disbanded SPI used to eliminate the "Indian problem" in Amazonia, current policies appear to be serving the dual purposes of resource extraction and the elimination of Indians, cloaked in the rhetoric of *development*.

The area along the northern border contains almost 25% of Brazil's Indian population. Here, the military authorities have full control over regional decisions, including land use and Indian policy. The concurrence of military bases and Indian lands in the area appears far from random. In fact, where perhaps half the land of this Calha Norte region is Indian territory, 13 out of 18 military bases have been established in or adjacent to Indian areas, and only 1 in 13 airstrips lies outside Indian land (CIMI 1986), (see Figure 6.1). Similarly, mining projects have an incredible propensity to fall within Indian occupied lands, as in the Waimiri-Atroari Reserve. The effects of mining are disastrous to the forest ecosystems, usually stripping away the forest and soil cover to expose the minerals of the subsoils (Grainger 1980). The numbers of miners attracted to new strikes often overwhelm the Indian populations of the areas, and conflict and disease lead to extensive decimations of Indian communities. Currently, at a goldstrike

Figure 6.1: Military posts and indigenous lands in Calha Norte

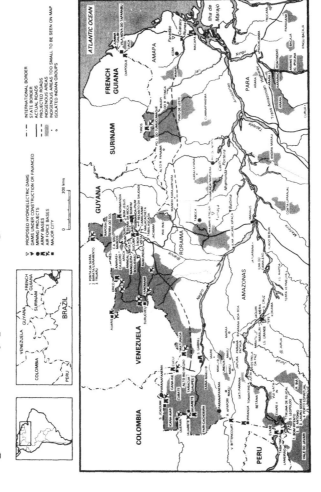

Source: CIMI 1986

within Yanomami territory in Roraima state, miners out-
number the Indian population by three to one, *inside the
reserve* (Anjudar 1988).

The Ecumenical Centre for Documentation and
Information (CEDI) in São Paulo has mapped overlays
of areas of official mining projects and indigenous lands.
Licences for mining operations have been granted or are
being processed for 13 indigenous territories in Amazonas
and 24 in Para. In Amazonas, the total area of land to be
conceded to mining is equal to almost a third of the total
area of the territories affected. In Para, over a quarter of the
affected territories will be given over to mining. In Rondonia
and Roraima nearly half of the territories "coinciding" with
mining concessions will be affected (see Table 6.1).

Table 6.1: Legal mining in Indian territories

State	Permits within reserves	Requests in process	Reserve area (ha)	Total area affected (ha)	Area affected %
Amazonas	38	418	13,139,550	4,011,651.9	31
Amapa	7	98	984,349	735,351.0	75
Maraba	13	30	1,103,349	292,014.5	27
Mato Grosso	40	69	2,691,900	626,192.6	23
Para	219	357	16,709,876	4,393,869.6	26
Rondonia	163	124	4,940,451	2,240,476.8	45
Roraima	80	589	12,809,331	5,335,169.2	42
TOTAL	560	1,685	52,378,806	17,634,725.5	34

Source: CEDI 1988

In short, it becomes clear that the protection offered by
Indian reserves is easily revoked in the interests of economic
development. At best, the real goals of Amazonian development neglect to consider the rights and welfare of the indigenous peoples. At worst, the evidence of excessive involvement

of government and private enterprise in indigenous territories represents an intentional elimination of the "primitive" elements of Brazil's Amazonia, in order to make way for an industrialized nation.

The plans for construction of hydroelectric dams on the Amazon waterways reveal similar patterns to the "coincidental" impacts of these other forms of development. Eletrobras itself points out that Indian communities "tend to occur with frequency" in the areas of planned hydroelectric projects (Viveros de Castro and Andrade 1988). In particular, the Xingu Complex is planned to develop and inundate one of the most isolated areas remaining in Amazonia, home to the most extensive Indian populations remaining in the country. Approximately 35,000 indigenous peoples occupy the area to be affected by the dams (International Rivers Network 1989). The execution of this one project will see to the acculturation or extermination of one of the greatest strongholds of Indian peoples and cultures remaining in Brazil.

Recognizing the opposition such action is likely to provoke, Eletrobras is extremely frugal with the information it reveals about the projects at Xingu and the reality behind the 2010 Plan. The Plan states: "The Sector will assure open access to information of public interest about its activities, permitting the supervision by the society over its functioning." However, obtaining access to the government's plans for projects in the initial phases of implementation is extremely difficult. In the actions of the Kayapo discussed in Chapter 5, it was not until the chiefs carried their protest to the United States that they discovered the actual stage of development that the Kararao Dam had reached. The Kayapo were, in fact, not alerted at all about the plans for construction, even as the infrastructure was being established in 1987 (Kaiapo 1988b). The dossier released by the Pro-Indian Commission (CPI) was designed specifically to fill this gap of information distribution on the part of the government planners.

International access to information on the dams is equally difficult. Organizations seeking to obtain the plans from the financing institutions, such as the World Bank, have had their attempts to procure such information systematically turned down. World Bank policy denies the citizens of the financing countries access to information about a borrowing nation's development plans. Additionally, when plans for projects are released, information is often omitted or contradicted by other government sources. The acquisition of accurate information becomes too complex to enable the majority of the population to pursue more than the most basic questions about the dams.

The 2010 Plan lists 31 dams to be built in the northern region, presumably encompassing all plans for the Amazonian waterways. Yet this assumption is not verified, as the Plan fails to provide a map defining the regions of North, Northeast, Southeast, South and Centre-west. Also, the total of 31 hydro-projects listed does not include the already constructed Tucurui or Balbina Dams; reference to these projects is not made until much later in the document. Most significantly, the CPI dossier presents a list released by Eletrobras only a year earlier which identifies 79 hydroelectric dams to be constructed in the Amazon basin. A comparison of the two lists reveals only 20 dams in common and this discrepancy potentially more than doubles the number of dams to be built on the Amazon's rivers. Further omissions in the 2010 Plan include the failure to present figures for the total area to be flooded by the dams. The CPI dossier reveals an estimate for the Xingu Complex of 18,000 km^2 with the filling of all six reservoirs, an area greater in size than the state of Massachusetts.

The symbolism of the development of the Brazilian nation is one of the most difficult hurdles to overcome in a unified resistance to Amazonian development policy. The drive of the government agencies and officials to develop Amazonia has been strengthened by an ideal which dictates that undeveloped land has no value. Discourses on the benefits of development versus the costs incurred in environmental and human degradation come to a standstill at the insistence of Brazil's need for development. Government rhetoric insists that the solution to many social problems, foremost among them being Brazil's foreign debt, is in industrial production and development. Offered very much like the "American Dream", development becomes "blind", progressing for its own sake. The majority of the population which does not directly feel the effects of the development projects, feels instead the promise for better living and national pride. The picture painted of development by the government instils a hope for what it could offer and discourages opposition as "un-Brazilian" or subversive.

An extreme example of this was recently demonstrated by the Malaysian government, similar to Brazil in its drive for export industries and in its treatment of the native peoples. Here, government logging concessions on indigenous lands in the rainforests of Sarawak have threatened the Penan tribe. The response of the Penan has been to block the logging roads with human barricades in order to stop the transport of timber and bar further entrance to their lands. The Malaysian government arrested 43 of the Penan for these actions in 1987, and an additional 81 were arrested in January 1989. A press release issued by the Prime Minister claims that the blockaders were Penan imposters hired by foreign timber companies to force Malaysia out of the world market (Rainforest Action Network 1988). According to the Malaysian government, the Penan support network which has responded internationally has been manipulated by this corporate manoeuvre.

Brazil similarly contends that the international environmental and human rights movement is a conspiracy to cripple the nation's economy. In the week preceding the voting on Indian rights in the Brazilian Constitution a series of conservative articles made headline news in the newspaper *O Estado de São Paulo*. The supporters of the indigenous rights clauses were denounced for engaging in a "Conspiracy against Brazil", intended to undermine Brazil's sovereignty in Amazonia (Maybury-Lewis 1989). Whether the "conspiracy" theory was inspired by extreme national paranoia or by one of the nation's largest mining firms (Paranapenama), as is suspected, the message is clear.

Supporting Amazonia's environment and peoples over the goals of development is labelled as subversive.

It is important to note that Brazil's development plans leave no room for considerations of compatibility with the ecosystem. The ideology rejects the concept of sustainable development, which suggests a compromise with the environment. Sustainability is only desirable if it can be translated into economic terms. The goal of development is not to sustain the forest, but rather to replace it with an industrialized nation. The elimination of the Amazon's "jungles" and its people is not an accidental consequence of development, but the realization of a carefully executed goal.

Apart from dissuading opposition from those outside Amazonia, or from the people not directly affected by the negative impacts of industrial hydro-development, the Brazilian government more strongly suppresses opposition from the affected peoples within the region. Prior to the new democracy, the primary deterrent to resistance may well have been the fear of retaliation by the authorities or by the wealthy élite. Today, there is still good reason for this fear to predominate and stifle resistance. As many as 90 Brazilians and Indians were assassinated in 1988 for their opposition to government policies or private landowners (Amnesty International 1988a; 1988b; 1989). One of the few to be reported in the American newspapers was the murder of Chico Mendes, president of Acre's rubber-tappers' union and an internationally known environmental advocate.

A further deterrent to opposition has been imposed as a result of the planning which went into colonizing Amazonia. In every phase of Amazonian development, government plans were laid out and functions were executed by regionally implanted agencies. Many people of Amazonia are still largely dependent on local government agencies to meet many of their basic needs, or to ensure legal rights to land and services. Without aid from these agencies, the peoples of Amazonia would have failed to withstand many of the relocations and marginalizations suffered as a result of the region's "integration". Most of these agencies are small subdivisions of larger government bodies; the Indian agency FUNAI is a subdivision of the Department of the Interior. As such they are concerned primarily with the promotion of development. In this way the Amazonian populations are effectively subordinated to the state, as a result of their dependencies. In order to continue receiving the "benefits" of government social programmes, they must co-operate with the system at a functional level. The dependence on government aid or services has undermined the ability or willingness of many of the local people to oppose the projects introduced into their areas.

Included in the strategies of the Brazilian government to dissipate opposition to Amazonian development projects is that of the "depoliticization" of the issues of human rights and social justice. In its discussions of the impacts of hydroelectric projects, Eletrobras relegates the social and human impacts to a category of *environmental* concerns, a less controversial issue in the Brazilian consciousness. Specifically, the environmental analysis of a project is determined by its impact on the "physical, biological, and socio-economic resources in its area of influence" (Viveros de Castro and Andrade 1988). "Socio-economic" effects refer to the impacts of development on the peoples of the area. By making this concern a component of the environmental question, Eletrobras makes clear how little importance it attributes to the local peoples in its planning considerations.

In discussing the "socio-economic" aspect of environmental effects, Eletrobras continues: "Three environmental components have proven to be particularly important for the planning of the hydroelectric works. The indigenous communities, the rural and urban populations, and the political leaders of the region affected by the reservoir." The great differences between the rural and urban populations are ignored, but the importance of the role the local political leaders play in facilitating or impeding a dam is clearly emphasized. The priorities of Eletrobras are made apparent through their view of the people as part of the environment of the dam, and by the categorical divisions drawn between the people themselves. The suggestion of political leaders as a separate entity from the other sectors of the population highlights them as a class to be considered separately, a necessary distinction in order to realize development goals successfully. Yet, they are still only an "environmental" aspect, in no way a definitive block to the government's plans for the dams.

In other documents released by Eletrobras, minimizing the importance of the people to be affected is repeated. Viveros de Castro and Andrade (1988) point out that in the discussions about the dams and the people to be affected, the places of the object and the subject are reversed. Eletrobras discusses the projects considering the dam as the *subject*, with the environment being the environment of the dam. The people in the area of the dam become the *objects*, passive reactors to the dam's construction. This point of view is exemplified in Eletrobras's discussions of the occurrence of dams and indigenous communities in the same locations, as has been discussed with reference to mining and military operations. Viveros de Castro and Andrade write: "We read that the indigenous communities 'occur with frequency' in the areas of hydroelectric projects – when the case appears to be that the hydroelectric dams 'occur with frequency' in indigenous areas." They describe the transference of the people affected to the place of objects as an example of the use of *concept manipulation* to deny the affected peoples their rights in the decisions about the dam. "It is not surprising that the process of making decisions regarding the planning and execution of the large hydroelectric dams completely defaults the social sectors affected: they do not consult the objects."

Brazilian energy policies in Amazonia aim to take resources away from the use of local peoples, and export them to the centres of industrial and political power. National development is designed not to benefit, but to exploit Amazonia. The peoples of the region can only impede this process or contribute to it by serving as a labour force. The resistance to hydroelectric development projects is in many respects a movement to establish the rights and worths of peoples, regardless of their utility to the government's plans for national development. The demands of Amazonians to halt colonialist policies is a demand for establishing social and political equalities for Amazonians. More than a struggle over specific energy projects, the movement against hydroelectric dams is a struggle for national political and social restructuring.

The recent advances in local-level initiatives to block or re-negotiate national development projects serve as testimony to a long history of regional abuses in the areas of hydroelectric constructions. The continuation of local em powerment in decision making, while strengthening alliances among affected sectors, may lead to choices for land use and the establishment of policies which could actually raise the quality of life and promote the self-determination of the Amazonian people. The development policies of the national Brazilian government are aimed at an entirely different goal.

The strategies used by Eletrobras to dissipate opposition suggest that the government does not consequentially marginalize native peoples and destroy the environment. Rather, the systematic elimination of the perceived barriers to development is intentional, if unstated, policy. "The environmental policy of the State, in sum, is a clear depoliticization of the environment, part of an offensive ideology that sees to the political facilitation of the *grandes projectos* in Amazonia" (Viveros de Castro and Andrade 1988).

7. PROSPECTS FOR THE FUTURE

The need to establish a more equitable social and political system in Brazil is necessary for the achievement of any significant change in development policy. The goals and ideals of the present national government subvert any real "development" for Brazil's poor and marginalized classes. The impacts which current policies are having and will continue to have on the peoples and environments of Amazonia are extreme. The view of Amazonia as a land to be tapped for uses determined by a centralized, authoritarian government effectively relegates Amazonia to being a colony of Brazil, rather than an integral part of the nation. Having discussed the attempts various opposing sectors of society are making to resist current development policies, it is necessary to determine what new, more responsible directions development may follow or, more specifically, the appropriate role for any future developments to be undertaken in Amazonia. Critical to an acceptable development policy are

- the benefits to be derived by the people directly affected; and
- the maintenance and care for an ecologically stable environment.

Alternatives

Several alternatives have been considered for national energy production, but, for reasons of resource and technology availability, not all of them are appropriate to Brazil (Rosa and Schaffer 1988). The replacement of imported petroleum is essential to the nation's economy, as Brazil's level of debt necessitates the minimization of costly import products. The cost of transporting petroleum to the distant frontiers in Brazil inflates its price above the already high price of oil on the international market. During the oil crisis of the 1970s, Brazil developed *proalcool*, an ethanol developed from sugar cane which, with adjustments to automobile engines, substituted for petroleum, replacing a portion of the import demand as cars could be run on this domestically produced fuel. A redefinition of the role of *proalcool* in other industries and uses is one option for alternative energy production in Brazil. However, the production of *proalcool* was accomplished by the use of large tracts of land for growing sugar cane, a strategy which has had its own problematic environmental and social impacts.

The natural resources available for energy production include coal deposits, especially in the South. In view of the quality and extent of Brazil's coal resources this option could potentially provide only a small contribution to a national energy solution, but it is one of several means available which together could form a consortium of energy options. Similarly, the use of biomass energy production could provide limited energy supplies, if carefully disciplined methods are used. On a decentralized scale, with disciplined methods of utilization, Rosa and Schaffer (1988) consider firewood fuel an important and viable source of rural energy. They specify as guidelines for firewood plantations the use of low-fertility areas which will not interfere with food-crop production (as opposed to the types of areas used for sugar-cane alcohol production), and note the damaging effects of producing single-species stands, such as eucalyptus plantations.

More than the previous two options, natural gas is seen as one of the most promising sources of energy for Brazil's future. Large reserves are known in the South, and with more precise studies of available potential in the North, and carefully formulated local policies for its utilization, gas may make an important contribution to Brazil's fuel resources. Other options such as solar energy are reserved as prospects for the future, as the technologies for their utilization are currently considered unavailable to Brazil (Rosa and Schaffer 1988).

Among the most responsible options for augmenting the Brazilian energy supply are the development of small hydro-power alternatives and energy-conservation improvements. With reference to small hydroelectric benefits, Rosa and Schaffer point out the much lower costs of construction as compared to large hydro-power projects, and the shorter amount of time required for implementation, allowing the benefit of greater flexibility in government planning. Hydroelectric energy could be provided as needed rather than relying on the current long-range predictions of demand which are required for large hydroelectric constructions. The resulting environmental impacts are much milder in the case of small hydroelectric projects and, with the use of "appropriate" technologies, environmental disturbance can be minimized.

Almost all regions of Brazil still have potential sites for small-scale hydro-development, while the large projects rely on the transfer of the energy produced over great distances. Rather than impoverishing the areas where large schemes are implemented for the sake of development in distant regions, small hydro-projects could promote regional development, manageable on a scale compatible with a stable ecosystem. However, the current government's interests have been demonstrated to lie in industrial development in Brazil's power centres, not in regional rural improvements, and so little attention is given to small-scale hydroelectric energy production.

INPA (the National Institute for Amazon Research) and the Energy Company of Amazonas have invested in research on small hydro-development on a rural, appropriate-technology scale. Virtually no support has been forthcoming from the federal holding agencies, as the interests of Eletrobras favour developing large hydroelectric projects for export and industrial uses. Since all funding for energy development falls under the jurisdiction of Eletrobras, no money has been available for the construction of the small projects (Handa 1988). The rural areas of Amazonas remain largely dependent upon petroleum, imported at great cost from the South. The centralized control over development policy makes it impossible to formulate regional energy projects without national government support.

The prospects for energy conservation have been given even less attention than the development of small-scale hydroelectric projects. Goods and industrial equipment domestically produced in Brazil are low in energy efficiency compared to current international standards (Rosa and Schaffer 1988). Investment in research and improvements in the production of high-efficiency equipment could result in significant energy savings, so that the country's current energy production could enable greater productivity than it does at present.

No single one of the possible alternative energy sources presented here is capable of replacing large hydroelectric projects to meet the energy-production goals Eletrobras has proposed for 2010. However, a combination of these strategies, augmented by a strict programme of enhanced energy efficiency and conservation, would serve to replace the construction of several of the most damaging of the energy sector's proposed projects.

In considering the demands beyond those which can be met with social and environmental equity, it becomes necessary to ask if the production of further energy is truly necessary or justifiable. If more energy is required to promote development than can be responsibly supplied, is the development worth the costs? In fact, the demands for development may even lead to the rejection of the alternatives proposed as contrary to its inherent goals.

Where viable alternatives for responsible development are available and are acceptable to environmentalists, the rural poor and indigenous communities, it cannot be assumed that they will be adopted by the Brazilian government. It has become clear that the removal of the forest and of the Indian is part of the developed ideal Brazil has set for itself. The sustainability and preservation of the elements of Amazonia which Brazil wants buried will not easily be incorporated into its development plans. The words of an Amazonian cattle rancher reflect this attitude: "The United States solved this problem with its army. They killed lots of Indians. Today everything is quiet there and the country is respected around the world" (Silva 1984).

Somewhat different from *responsible* development, and carrying connotations of social equity, is the concept of *sustainable* development. Sustainable development refers to means of exploiting natural resources in a renewable manner. However, the concept in no way implicitly provides for social equality or justice, as is sometimes assumed. Large corporations or government projects may establish sustainable programmes for the exploitation of resources which do not provide for integrated ecosystems or the preservation of economically expendable species. Indian lands may be violated and local people may no longer have access to or benefit from certain resources. Yet, if a project is properly planned, it may still be "sustainable". To look to sustainable development as the solution to the Amazon crisis is misguided unless the idea is accompanied by careful and constant provision for the conservation and democratization of resources. Plans such as the highly acclaimed Bruntdland Commission Report (1988) and the Tropical Forestry Action Plan (1987), both intended as plans for natural/social resource management, are equally misleading, as their solutions to social equity or land rights are delivered "top down". The people affected have no part in the planning. Ultimately, the focus of these plans is the servicing, albeit responsibly/sustainably, of the international market.

The crux of the question, "Is the development worth it?", from the view of Eletrobras, lies ultimately with its effect on the national economy. Until a strengthening of the Amazonian peoples and environmental values occurs, decisions concerning development policy will continue to be made by the federal levels of the government. In encouraging Brazil to re-evaluate the effects of its development policies on its *stated* goals, several recent "revelations" have been incorporated into public understanding. The debts incurred by Brazil in implementing its development programmes are proving to be unserviceable. The expected returns on development programmes have not been forthcoming, and the resultant economic crisis continues to escalate. At this point in time, loans are being taken or forceably incurred by Brazil through International Monetary Fund restructuring programmes, in order to pay the interest on previous debts.

A great number of the programmes implemented with borrowed money have failed. Cattle ranching, hydroelectric construction, road building, colonization – all have experienced failures and resulted in a higher level of national debt than existed before their role in economic "development". With respect to hydroelectric projects in Amazonia, two of the three works constructed have been admitted to be mistakes by the Brazilian government (*New York Times* 1989a). In short, the development plans of the national government to dam the Amazonian rivers and strengthen Brazil's economy appear to be failing in their intended purposes, as well as in the needs for cultural and physical survival of the Amazonian peoples and the stability of the environment.

Strengthening the resistance

The strengthening of the environmental, social justice, and Indian rights movements in Brazil is essential to the bringing about of change in national energy development policy.

Several related elements are weakening the resistance to current projects and they threaten to dissipate the impacts of previous accomplishments. Foremost among these is fragmentation; there is a vital need to establish alliances between the varied sectors affected by current policy. While initial reasons for opposing government energy-development plans may be vastly different, alliances can be made to attain a mutually desired goal.

The tendency to exclude or criticize other social or political groups is exceedingly widespread in Brazil. Ecologists are criticized as being too specialist, and may suffer from class barriers when it comes to understanding the struggles of rural peasants. They in turn discredit other groups for lacking a systematic approach or being limited in education. Environmentalists are labelled as being unconcerned with people, for their focus is on the forests and wildlife. At times this complaint is sadly appropriate. Organizations of rural peasants often exclude the Indian people as not being a "Brazilian" concern or as being racially inferior to themselves. This antagonism between the Brazilian peasant and Indian has been exacerbated by the government's colonization programmes. Often, the Indian people are simply dismissed as inferior, a primitive race which must fall in the face of progress. Various counter-political groups, such as the Workers' Party and the Brazilian Socialist Party, are marginalized by being labelled special-interest groups. They frequently have the additional problem of being unable to resolve underlying ideological conflicts. Assistance from local government agencies is often suspected as being a scheme for the agencies' own economic benefit, or as being concerned only with profits.

The fragmentation of potentially compatible interests resulting from such exclusivity frustrates developmental and social reform. The formation of alliances between sectors and organizations may prove the means of strengthening individual positions in a region where so many are marginalized by the more powerful interests of the federal state.

In recent years, tentative experiments in aligning goals have emerged. The first of these is the proposal for "extractive reserves" in the state of Acre, proposed by rubber-tapper leader Chico Mendes. Rubber tapping is a sustainable use of forest resources long practised by rural Amazonians. The National Rubbertappers Council and the Union of Indigenous Nations have jointly proposed a system of non-private extractive rubber reserves forming protective "green belts" around demarcated indigenous territories. The project would be mediated by an Amazon Forest Peoples Alliance, equally represented by rubber tappers and Indian leaders. The plan would maintain forest habitats, as needed by rubber–tapping and traditional communities; provide non-exploitive income for the Amazonian Brazilians (the plan calls for excluding the exploitative middle-men in the rubber trade); and protect Indian lands (Survival International 1987). Schwartzman and Allegretti (1987) note that "Extractive reserves offer not only a solution to land conflicts and conservation of the forest, but a development alternative as well", and report that the World Bank has endorsed the project as a viable conservation and development alternative.

Other innovative alliances have been made between conservation and economic interests; one such plan is under discussion by the International Tropical Timber Organization which is researching ways to harvest tropical hardwoods sustainably from rainforest reserves. Following a meeting in Brazil in 1988, the *Washington Post* reported that:

> Producers and consumers of the world's rapidly dwindling supply of tropical timber have begun a serious dialogue aimed at conserving rainforests now being destroyed at the rate of 100 acres per minute. . . . At the core of the debate lies the concept of sustainably managed forest reserves that can yield successive crops of timber, rubber, nuts, fibers, and medicinal plants over centuries, without necessarily evicting forest or tribal dwellers.

> (*Washington Post* 1988)

Another example is currently being mediated by Cultural Survival, an organization formed to aid in the defence of native peoples' rights internationally. The harvesters of brazil nuts in Amazonia are following the example of the rubber tappers and arranging to bypass the exploitative middlemen in marketing their products. Cultural Survival is arranging the transport of their brazil nuts to the United States for sale, until the harvesters can take responsibility for transport themselves (Clay, 1989). The first commercial product of this arrangement, a brazil-nut candy brittle called Rainforest Crunch, reached the US market in 1990. While caution has to be taken in an exploitative world market, these initiatives represent rare alliances of interests, upon whose successes many struggles for conservation and human rights may depend.

One of the most successful examples of alliances between varied sectors concerned with development plans is that formulated in reaction to the Xingu dams. The Kayapo have initiated an alliance of scientists, Indians, Amazonian Brazilians, international non governmental organizations (NGOs) and the concerns of multilateral lending institutions. Their case, outlined in Chapter 5, has been a landmark in the progress of the struggle for human and environmental considerations in Brazilian development policy. The Kayapo's most recent action has been to call a meeting of all Indian nations and supporters, and the concurrent building of a village on the site of the proposed Kararao Dam. The action represented the Amazonian resistance's most complete show of unity among the affected sectors to date. Traditionally warring or unacquainted Indian nations met for a week in Altamira to discuss a unified Indian resistance to Brazilian development. They were further strengthened by the participation of local Brazilians opposed to the dams, as well as by international environmental and human rights organizations prepared to act on the lead of local initiatives resulting from the meeting. The attention of the press put further pressure on the Brazilian government, and the public and private banks with loans under consideration to Brazil, to reform their policies. Two months later the World Bank withdrew its support for the dams, rejecting a request for $500 million from Brazil's energy department.

The extension of NGOs into Amazonia will help to strengthen resistance to nationally motivated development. The establishment of NGOs provides a tool for unified, popular influence and action, simultaneously forcing the government agencies to take a more dynamic role in meeting the needs and demands of the Amazonian people. Currently, the majority of NGOs working in Brazil, even on Amazonian issues, are based in the South of the country, far from the realities and problems of Amazonia. Without the infrastructure of existing organizations to provide an avenue of support and direction for opposition, the ability of the majority of Amazonians to act to influence policy is greatly weakened. The empowerment derived from the "strength in numbers", independent of government interference, is lacking. The current status and importance of NGOs is outlined by Landim:

> NGOs can become significant actors in achieving and guar-
> anteeing democracy in Latin America. The recent attempts to
> form more permanent networks of NGOs bolster the chances
> of becoming actors that count in the political and social
> relations among the countries of Latin America. . . . They
> are beginning to perceive the importance of coordinating
> their efforts in a more permanent fashion. Although there
> is clearly a trend in this direction, as of yet there are not
> specific results in terms of establishing these more formalized
> networks.
>
> (Landim 1987)

As most financial support for NGOs is provided by organizations in the "developed" countries, this strengthening calls for international co-operation. Financial constraints greatly impair the ability of the Amazonian people to organize effective resistance and develop alternative modes of meeting local demands.

The role of NGOs, both in Brazil and internationally can also play a great part in filling the gap of education. To influence policy-making in Brazil, and to influence foreign funding criteria internationally, environmental and developmental history education is essential to the formation of the values and knowledge of policy-makers and the public alike.

As long as Brazil treats Amazonia as its colony for raw materials, land-reform relief and energy, the undermining of the rights of the people and the integrity of the forest will continue. The current development policies and regional–federal state relations deny the people of low socio-political status the benefits of the land, and exploit natural resources to serve the élite, and foreign markets. An understanding of the US treatment of Brazil as an economic colony is also important in changing these internal Brazilian relationships and gaining a position of equality and independence for Amazonia. Through the collection of outstanding debts, international banks and governments further exacerbate Brazil's economic problems.

In order to gain a voice in the developmental, environmental and social decisions Brazil makes, the peoples of Amazonia will have to link their efforts and goals in a co-ordinated popular movement capable of challenging the power structures Brazil uses to repress the region today. With the initiation of the Xingu Dams resistance, an impetus has been given to other such movements to strengthen their organization. The democratization of information and public opposition from all affected sectors offers a timely opportunity to meet the challenge of a united resistance, and to form a network to protect the future needs of Amazonia.

EPILOGUE

My research in Brazil ended shortly after the charges were levied against Dr Darrell Posey under the Foreigners' Act. As general surveillance of foreigners increased, I was followed by a government van from Eletronorte, near my hotel in Manaus. The one-time environmental advocate, Roberto Zuazo, who introduced me to the subject of the dams, also followed me that evening, presumably to keep my activities under surveillance. I had never informed him of my whereabouts or contacted him in Brazil and, despite our previous acquaintance in the United States, he never approached me. When two police cars joined the already nerve-wracking entourage, I contacted a missionary whose phone number two bicyclists had given me a month before. "He's an American, and loves to have people for dinner. Go meet him." He may have got more than he bargained for when I arrived frantically, with all my bags in tow.

Padre Frederico was surprised by my story. "Ten years ago, this was common. But I didn't realize it was still happening." He welcomed me to stay, and drove me to the airport in the morning. I cannot thank him enough, for at least my piece of mind, and perhaps also my safety.

When I arrived in São Paulo, I discovered that a contact there had a file on Mr Zuazo. He wrote extensively against Indian and environmental groups, leading the public and international supporters to believe that they embezzled funds, and declaring them corrupt and useless. Additionally, a series of confusing articles connected him with a case in which an Indian activist was run over and almost killed. Several of my Brazilian contacts had met with similar "accidents", such as the road accident that led to facial reconstruction surgery for the president of the Indian Missionary Council. We also found that I had acquired documents not yet held by the Ecumenical Centre for Documentation and Information, perhaps the most thorough organization promoting public distribution of information in Brazil.

After exchanging information with CEDI, I left São Paulo for the United States. In Washington, DC, I shared my experiences and impressions with Congressmen, Treasury and the Agency for International Development (AID). When the photographs documenting my research were mailed by my photographer from Georgia to Washington, only an empty packet arrived. I returned to Massachusetts ready to sort through my material and begin writing. Two weeks later, a letter arrived from Roberto Zuazo. It entirely ignored the incident in Manaus and talked instead of art, finishing with "I'll see you soon." I never heard from him again.

Many of the subsequent events and acts of protest in Brazil alerted the international community to the dangers posed by the Amazonian dams. In March 1988, the Brazilian power sector loan being considered by the World Bank was rejected. The following article appeared in the *Boston Globe* on 12 April 1989, announcing the World Bank's decision.

APPENDIX: WORLD BANK REFUSES LOAN WHICH WOULD FUND AMAZONIAN DAMS

Reproduced by kind permission of The Boston Globe

In a move that could make 10 big dams in the Amazon basin unnecessary, the World Bank and the government of Brazil have quietly shelved a controversial $500 million energy loan and have begun talks on as much as $350 million in assistance for environmental protection and energy conservation, according to bank officials and Brazilian sources.

This shift marks a significant victory in the battle to save the Amazon rain forest and could represent an important precedent for the bank's energy lending to developing countries, say environmentalists and energy specialists.

"This is the first time that a big loan" for energy conservation "is in the works," said José Goldemberg, a Brazilian energy specialist, who developed the plan now under consideration by the bank. "This is a very important development." Before this, Goldemberg noted, "all the loans on the environment have been small loans, sort of an afterthought."

If this new loan sets a precedent for World Bank lending for energy projects elsewhere in the developing world, it could have a tremendous impact on the worldwide energy picture and the closely linked greenhouse problem, he said. "The World Bank," he noted, "is the main financing agent for power generation all over the world."

Goldemberg, who has attended several recent international meetings on the greenhouse problem, has warned that developing countries will be producing more greenhouse gases than the industrialized countries by 2000.

Up to now, according to Howard Geller of the American Council for an Energy-Efficient Economy, "the World Bank has not been greatly interested in end-use conservation. The bank has not funded one significant electricity conservation project."

If this loan to Brazil goes through, Geller said, "it's a very promising step in the right direction that could be a milestone for the World Bank and other funders."

Some US environmentalists remain skeptical that this shift on the Brazil loan represents a new departure on energy lending.

"The reorientation of this money is welcome," said David Wirth of the Natural Resources Defense Council, a national group that has been pushing environmental reforms in the World Bank. But so far, he noted, the proposed loan to Brazil "looks like an isolated case. It's not clear that the need for increased lending for end-use efficiency has penetrated the bank's culture."

Because of Brazil's extreme sensitivity to outside criticism regarding the destruction of the Amazon rain forest, bank officials were reluctant to discuss how this shift occurred or to say much about the ongoing discussions.

Peter Riddleberger, a bank spokesman, did confirm that the bank is considering a major energy conservation loan to Brazil.

According to other sources, the bank is considering a total sum of about $350 million. As currently conceived, roughly 75 per cent of this sum would be earmarked for an "environmental loan" that would provide funds to hire environmental professionals in the power ministry, the forestry ministry and other government agencies involved in the dams and other power developments. The object is to strengthen the environmental expertise in agencies that plan and evaluate power sector projects.

The other 25 per cent would go directly to improving energy efficiency by reducing losses in transmission or by directly improving the efficiency of the appliances or light bulbs that use the electricity, one bank source said.

Goldemberg, who is the former head of the São Paulo state utility, ascribes the Brazilian government's interest in energy efficiency to "a combination of virtue and necessity. The World Bank has been refusing to give them money for nuclear power stations and dams that have very serious environmental consequences."

Goldemberg added that he had been "pestering" the government for years to invest in energy efficiency instead of new dams because it makes economic as well as environmental sense.

If Brazil invested $8 billion to improve the energy efficiency of such electrical appliances as refrigerators and air conditioners, Goldemberg calculates that it could avoid spending $38 billion for big hydroelectric dams.

In general, he said, electrical appliances sold in Brazil use twice as much electricity as those sold in the United States. In fact, he noted, one Brazilian factory owned by a multinational company makes two models of air conditioners in an energy-efficient model for export to the United States and an electricity guzzler for the Brazilian market.

In the face of strong pressure from environmental and human rights groups, members of Congress and other critics, the bank had delayed a vote on the original loan package for more than a year.

Dianne Dumanoski, *The Boston Globe*, 12 April 1989

REFERENCES

A Critica (1987). "Hidrolétrica Balbina sob debate aberta", 26 August.

A Critica (1988). "Pesquisador acusa o erro de Balbina", 20 July.

Agricultural Workers Union (1988). Meeting at Cachoeira Morena, June.

Allen, R.N. (1972). "The Anchicaya Hydroelectric Project in Colombia: design and sedimentation problems", in *The Careless Technology* (New York: Natural History Press),/ pp. 318–42.

Amin, M.A. (1979). "Schistosomiasis in the Gezira", *Aquatic Weed Management* (Wad Medain: University of Gezira). Quoted by Nigel Pollard (1981). "The Gezira Scheme: a study in failure", *The Ecologist*, vol. 11, no. 1, January–February, p. 24. Cited in Edward Goldsmith and Nicholas Hildyard, (1984) *The Social and Environmental Effects of Large Dams* (San Francisco: Sierra Club Books), p. 83.

Amnesty International (1988a). *Brazil: Briefing* (New York: Amnesty International) September.

Amnesty International (1988b). *Brazil: Cases of Killings and Ill Treatment of Indigenous People* (New York: Amnesty International), November.

Amnesty International (1989). *Brazil: Open Targets for Assassination: A Policy of Government Negligence? (Summary)* (London: Amnesty International), January.

Anderson, Anthony and Darrell Posey (1987). "Indian reforestation", *Ciência Hoje*, vol. 6, no. 31, May, pp. 45–50.

Anjudar, Claudia (Director, Committee for the Creation of the Yanomami Park), (1988). Interview, 31 May.

Arnason, T., F. Uck, J Lambert, and R Hebda (1980). "Maya medicinal plants of San José Succotz, Belize", *Journal of Ethnopharmacology*, vol. 2, no. 4, pp. 345–64.

Barrow, Chris (1988). "The impact of hydroelectric development on the Amazonia environment: with particular reference to the Tucurui Project", *Journal of Biogeography*, vol. 15, pp. 67–78.

Bates, Henry Walter (1864). *The Naturalist on the River Amazon* (London: John Murray). In Roger Stone (1985), *Dreams of Amazonia* (New York: Penguin Books), p. 65.

Bondurant, D.C. and R.H. Livesey (1973). "Reservoir sedimentation studies", in W. C. Ackerman, G. F. White and E. B. Worthington (eds), *Man Made Lakes: Their Problems and Environmental Effects*, Geophysical Monographs no. 17 (Washington, DC: American Geophysical Union).

Brazilian Constitution – Civil Code (1966). Cited in Amnesty International (1988b), Appendix.

Brock, Glenio (Instituto do Desenvolvimento Econômico e Social do Para), (1988). Interview, 27 July.

Brown, A.W.A. and J.O. Deom (1973). "Health aspects of man made lakes", in W. C. Ackerman, G.F.White and E.B.Worthington (eds), *Man Made Lakes: Their Problems and Environmental Effects*, Geophysical Monographs no. 17 (Washington, DC: American Geophysical Union).

Brundtland (1987). Report to the World Commission on Environment and Development (London: Zed Books).

Bunker, Stephen G. (1985). *Underdeveloping the Amazon: Extraction, Unequal Exchange, and the Failure of the Modern State* (Chicago: University of Chicago Press).

Bunyard, Peter (1985). "World climate and tropical forest destruction", *The Ecologist*, vol. 15, no. 3, pp. 125–36.

Burns, Bradford E. (1970). *A History of Brazil* (New York: Columbia University Press).

Byrne, Louise (1989). "Word from the water", *Observer Magazine*, 19 November.

de Carvajal, Friar Gaspar (1554). Chronicles. Published in José Toribio Medina (1934), *The Discovery of the Amazon* (New York: American Geographical Society).

Carvalho, J.C. (1981). "The conservation of nature and natural resources in the Brazilian Amazon", *Revista Companhia Vale do Rio Doce*, no. 2, pp. 1-48. Cited in Thomas Lovejoy and Eneas Salati. "Precipitating change in Amazonia", in Emilio Moran (ed 1983), *The Dilemma of Amazonian Development* (Colorado: Westview Press).

Caufield, Catherine (1982). "Brazil, energy and the Amazon", *New Scientist*, October, pp. 240–43.

Caufield, Catherine (1984). *In the Rainforest* (Chicago: University of Chicago Press).

CEDI (Centro Ecumenical de Documentação e Informação), (1988). *Empressas de Mineração e Terras Indígenas na Amazonia* (São Paulo: CEDI/CONAGE).

CEDI (Centro Ecumenical de Documentação e Informação), (1989). "Indian rights in the new Brazilian constitution", *Cultural Survival Quarterly*, vol. 13, no. 1, pp. 6–12.

Chernela, Janet (Anthropologist, Cultural Survival), (1988). Personal communication, January.

CIMI (Conselho Indigenista Missionário), (1986). "Calha Norte: Segurança ou ameaça?" (Manaus: CIMI).

Clay, Jason (Research Director, Cultural Survival), (1989). Personal communication, April.

CNEC (Consorcio National de Engenheiros Consultores)/Eletronorte (1988). *Aspetos Gerais de UHE Kararao* (Brazil: Eletrobras).

Conhaft, Mário (Ecologist, INPA), (1988). Personal communication, June.

Correa, Suzanna (Journalist, *O Kaiapo*), (1988). Interview, 10 July.

Correa, Suzanna and Deputado Andrade (1988). Meeting of the Partido dos Trabalhadores (Workers' Party) and the Partido Socialista Brazileiro (Brazilian Socialist Party). Altamira, Brazil, 12 July.

CPI (Comissão Pro-Indio), (1988). *As Hidrelétricas do Xingu e os Povos Indígenas* (São Paulo, CPI).

Davis, Shelton (1977). *Victims of the Miracle: Development and the Indians of Brazil* (Cambridge: Cambridge University Press).

Deudney, Daniel (1981). Rivers of Energy: The hydropower potential (Washington, DC: Worldsatch Institute).

Drucker, Charles (1985). "Dam the Chico: Hydropower development and tribal resistance", *The Ecologist*, vol. 15, no. 4, pp. 149–57.

Eletrobras (no date). *UHE Balbina*, cartoon propaganda booklet.

Eletrobras (1987). *Plano 2010: Relatório Geral. Plano Nacional de Energia Elétrica: 1987/2010* (Rio de Janeiro: Ministry of Mines and Energy).

Eletronorte(undated). *UHE Balbina*, cartoon propaganda booklet.

Eletronorte (1988). *Estudos Xingu: Estudos de Viabilidade, UHE Kararao: EIA/RIMA* (Preliminar) (Brasilia: Eletrobras).

Eletronorte/CNEC (1988a). *Aspetos Gerais da UHE Kararao* (Brasil: Eletronorte).

Eletronorte/CNEC (1988b). *UHE Kararao: Estudos de Viabilidade: Panorama Atual* (Brasilia: Eletrobras).

Eletronorte/FUNAI (1988). *Waimiri-Atroari* (Brazil: Eletronorte).

Erwin, Terry L. (1982). Cited in T.L. Erwin (1988), "The tropical forest canopy", in E.O. Wilson, (ed.), *Biodiversity* (Washington, DC: National Academy Press).

Erwin, T. L. and J.C. Scott (1980). "Seasonal size pattern, trophic structure, and richness of Coleoptera in the tropical aboreal ecosystem: the fauna of the tree *Luehea seemannii triana* and planch in the canal zone of Panama", *Coleoptera Bulletin*, vol. 34, no. 3, pp. 305–22 (in ibid.).

Espenshade, Edward (ed.), (1986). *Goode's World Atlas* (Chicago: Rand McNally).

Fearnside, Phillip (1982). "Deforestation in the Brazilian Amazon: how fast is it occurring?" *Interciência*, vol. 7, no. 2, March/April.

Fearnside, Phillip (1985). "Agriculture in Amazonia", in Ghillean Prance and Thomas Lovejoy (eds.), *Key Environments: Amazonia* (Oxford: Pergamon Press), pp. 393–418.

Fearnside, Phillip (Ecologist, INPA), (1988). Interview, 22 June.

Gat, J.R., E. Matsui and E. Salati (1985). "The effects of deforestation on the water cycle in the Amazon basin: an attempt to reformulate the problem", *Acta Amazonica*, vol. 15, no. 34, September/December.

Glymph, Louis M. (1973). "Sedimentation of reservoirs", in W. C. Ackerman, G.F. White and E.B. Worthington, (eds) *Man Made Lakes: Their Problems and Environmental Effects*, Geophysical Monographs no. 17 (Washington, DC: American Geophysical Union).

Goldsmith, Edward and Nicholas Hildyard (1984). *The Social and Environmental Effects of Large Dams* (San Francisco: Sierra Club Books).

Goldsmith, Edward and Nicholas Hildyard (eds), (1986). *The Social and Environmental Effects of Large Dams. Vol. 2: Case Studies* (London: Wadebridge Ecological Centre).

Goodland, Robert (1978). *Environmental Assessment of the Tucuruí Hydroelectric Project* (Brasilia: Eletronorte). Cited in Edward Goldsmith and Nicholas Hildyard (1984), *The Environmental and Social Effects of Large Dams* (San Francisco: Sierra Club Books).

Goodland, Robert (1986). "Hydro and the environment: evaluating the tradeoffs", *Water Power and Dam Construction*, November.

Goulding, Michael (1985). "Forest fishes of the Amazon", in Ghillean Prance and Thomas Lovejoy (eds), *Key Environments: Amazonia* (Oxford: Pergamon Press), pp. 267–76.

Grainger, Alan (1980). "The state of the world's tropical forests", *The Ecologist*, vol. 10, pp. 6–54.

Handa, Jirson (Companhia Elétrica da Amazonas), (1988). Personal communication, June.

Hartshorn, Gary S. (1980). "Neotropical forest dynamics", *Biotropica*, vol. 12, supplement, pp. 23–30.

Hecht, Suzanna (1985). "Cattle ranching in the Eastern Amazon: environmental and social implications", in Emilio Moran (ed.), *The Dilemma of Amazonian Development* (Colorado: Westview Press).

Hecht, Suzanna and Alexander Cockburn (1989). *The Fate of the Forest* (London: Verso).

Herrera, Rafael (1985). "Nutrient cycling in Amazonian forests", in Ghillean Prance and Thomas Lovejoy (eds), *Key Environments: Amazonia* (Oxford: Pergamon Press), pp. 95–105.

Hunter, J. M., L. Rey and D. Scott (1982). "Man made lakes and man made diseases", *Social Science and Medicine*, vol. 16, pp. 1127–45.

IDESP (Instituto do Desenvolvimento Económico e Social do Pará). Files (Belem, Brazil).

International Rivers Network (1989). "On the move against the Xingu Dams", *World Rivers Review*, vol. 4, no. 1, January/February.

Jordan, Carl F. (1985). "Soils of the Amazon rainforest", in Ghillean Prance and Thomas Lovejoy (eds), *Key Environments: Amazonia* (Oxford: Pergamon Press).

Jordan, Carl F. (1987). In MAREWA (1987), *Balbina: Ameaça e Destruição na Amazonia* (Manaus: MAREWA).

Kaiapo, Paulinho Paiakan (1988a). Presentation at the First International Congress of Ethnobiology, Belem, Brazil, 23 July.

Kaiapo, Paulinho Paiakan (Kayapo Political Chief), (1988b). Interview, 24 July.

Lal, R. (1987). *Tropical Ecology and Physical Edaphology* (New York: Wiley and Sons).

Landim, Leilah (1987). "Non-governmental organizations in Latin America", *World Development*, vol. 15, supplement, pp. 29–38.

Lange, Alberto (Social Worker, Eletronorte), (1988). Interview, 27 June.

Lombana, Abdon Cortes (1975). "Soil capability and management in Columbian Amazonia and Orinoquia", in IUCN, *The Use of Ecological Guidelines for Development in the American Humid Tropics*, Proceedings of International Meeting held in Caracas, 20–22 February 1974 (Old Woking, England: Unwin Brothers Ltd, Gresham Press).

Mahar, Dennis J. (1989). *Government Policies and Deforestation in Brazil's Amazon Region* (Washington, DC: World Bank).

MAREWA (Movimento de Apoio a Resistencia Waimiri–Atroari), (1987), *Balbina: Ameaça e Destruicão na Amazonia* (Manaus: MAREWA).

Maybury-Lewis, David (1989). "Indians in Brazil: the struggle intensifies", *Cultural Survival Quarterly*, vol. 13, no. 1, pp. 2–5.

Meggers, Betty J. (1971). *Amazonia: Man and Culture in a Counterfeit Paradise* (Chicago: Aldine Publishing).

Monosowski, Elizabeth (1986). "Brazil's Tucurui Dam: development at environmental cost", in Edward Goldsmith and Nicholas Hildyard (eds), *The Social and Environmental Effects of Large Dams. Vol. 2: Case Studies* (London: Wadebridge Ecological Centre).

Moran, Emilio (1983). "Growth without development: past and present development efforts in Amazonia", in Emilio Moran (ed.), *The Dilemma of Amazonian Development* (Colorado: Westview Press), pp. 3–23.

Myers, Norman (1984). *The Primary Source* (New York: W.W. Norton and Co.).

Nemec, J. (1973). "Interactions between reservoirs and the atmosphere and its hydrometeorological elements", in W. C. Ackerman, G. F. White and E. B. Worthington, (eds), *Man Made Lakes: Their Problems and Environmental Effects*, Geophysical Monographs no. 17 (Washington, DC: American Geophysical Union).

New York Times (1989a). "Brazil's quest for energy puts more pressure on the Amazon", 12 March.

New York Times (1989b). "As Brazilian election nears, magic of democracy wanes", 21 March.

Nyrop, Richard (ed.), (1983). *Brazil: A Country Study* (Washington, DC: The American University (Foreign Area Studies)).

Obi, M.E. (1982). "Runoff and soil loss from an oxisol in Southeastern Nigeria under various management practices", *Agricultural Water Management*, vol. 5, pp. 193–203.

O Estado do São Paulo (1988). "O Escalando da Hidréletrica Balbina", 31 July.

O Liberal (1988a). "Autoritarismo seria causa do processo de expulsão", 26 July.

O Liberal (1988b). "Indios se instalam no Posto da Funai em Imperatriz", 28 July.

Parsons, James J. (1975). "The changing nature of the New World tropical forests since European colonization", in IUCN, *The Use of Ecological Guidelines for Development in the American Humid Tropics* (Old Woking, England: Unwin Brothers Ltd, Gresham Press), pp. 28–38.

Pimenta-Neves, Antonio (Public Information, World Bank), (1989). Personal communication, April.

Plotkin, Mark (1988). "The outlook for new agricultural and industrial products from the Tropics", in E.O. Wilson (ed.) *Biodiversity* (Washington, DC: National Academy Press), pp. 106–16.

Posey, Darrell A. (1985). "Indigenous management of tropical forest ecosystems: the case of the Kayapo Indians of the Brazilian Amazon", *Agroforestry Systems*, vol. 3, pp. 139–58.

Prance, Ghillean (1985). "The changing forests", in Ghillean Prance and Thomas Lovejoy (eds), *Key Environments: Amazonia* (Oxford: Pergamon Press), pp. 146–65.

Prelazia do Xingu. Files (Belem, Brazil).

Rainforest Action Network (1988). Press Release on Malaysian Penan, San Francisco.

Raven, Peter (1988). "Our diminishing tropical forests", in E.O. Wilson (ed.), *Biodiversity* (Washington, DC: National Academy Press), pp. 119–22.

Roosevelt, Theodore (1919). *Through the Brazilian Wilderness* (New York: Charles Scribner's Sons).

Rosa, L.P. and R. Schaffer (1988). "Propostas alternativas da política energética Brasileira", in Leinal A. Santos and Lucia M.M. de Andrade (eds), *As Hidrelétricas do Xingu e as Povos Indígenas* (São Paulo: Comissão Pro-Indio).

Rural Agricultural Workers' Union (1988). Meeting at Cachoeira Morena, Amazonas, June

Salo, J., R. Kalliola, I. Hakkinen, Y. Makinen, P. Niemala, M. Puhakka, P. D. Coley (1986). "River dynamics and the diversity of Amazon lowland forest", *Nature*, vol. 322, pp. 254–58.

Santilli, Marcio (1989). "The Calha Norte Project: military guardianship and frontier policy", *Cultural Survival Quarterly*, vol. 13, no. 1, pp. 42–3.

Santos, Leinal Ayer O. and Lucia Andrade (eds), (1988). *As Hidrelétricas do Xingu e as Povos Indígenas* (São Paulo: Comissao Pro-Indio).

Santos, M. (Engineer, Eletronorte), (1988). Personal communication, June.

Schwade, Egydio. In print. *Os Grandes Empreendimentos na Amazonia e seu Custo Social.*

Schwade, Egydio (Director, MAREWA), (1988). Interview, 23 June.

Schwartzman, Stephen and Mary Helena Allegretti (1987). "Extractive production in the Amazon and the rubber tappers' movement" (Washington, DC: Environmental Defense Fund).

Silva (1984). Quoted in Catherine Caufield (1984). *In the Rainforest* (Chicago: University of Chicago Press), p. 104.

SOPREN, Sociadade de Preservacao aos Recursos Naturais e Culturais da Amazonia (1988).

Stark, Nellie M., and Carl F. Jordan (1978). "Nutrient retention by the root mat of an Amazonian rain forest", *Ecology*, vol. 59, no. 3, pp. 434–7.

Stone, Roger D. (1985). *Dreams of Amazonia* (New York: Penguin Books).

Survival International (1987). "Amazon alliance", *Survival International News*, no. 17.

Tasker (1987). In Peter Raven (1988), "We're killing our world", Address to the American Association for the Advancement of Science, Chicago, 14 February.

Terena, Marcos (1988). Presentation at the First International Congress of Ethnobiology (Belem, Brazil), 23 July.

Tosi, Joseph A. (1974). "Some relationships of climate to economic development in the Tropics", in IUCN, *The Use of Ecological Guidelines for Development in the American Humid Tropics* (Old Woking, England: Gresham Press, Unwin Brothers Ltd).

Tropical Forestry Action Plan (1985). Committee on Forest Development in the Tropics (Rome: FAO).

Uhl, Christopher (1988). "Restoration of degraded lands in the Amazon Basin", in E.O. Wilson (ed.), *Biodiversity* (Washington, DC: National Academy Press), pp. 326–32.

Vesilind, Pritt J. (1987), "Brazil: moments of promise and pain". *National Geographic*, vol. 171, no. 3, March.

Viana, Camil (Director, (Sociedade de pare a Preservação dos Recursos Naturais e Culturais da Amazonia) (1988). Interview, 27 July.

Viveros de Castro, Eduardo, and Lucia M.M. de Andrade (1988). "Hidrelétricas do Xingu: O estado contra as sociadades indigenas", in Leinal A. Santos and Lucia M.M. de Andrade (eds), *As Hidrelétricas do Xingu e As Povos Indígenas* (São Paulo: Comissão Pro-Indio).

Wagley, Charles (1953). *Amazon Town: A Study of Man in the Tropics* (New York: The MacMillan Co.).

Washington Post (1988). "Timber producers, users talk of saving forests", 23 July.

Wilson, E.O. (1988). "The current state of biological diversity", in E. O. Wilson (ed.), *Biodiversity* (Washington, DC: National Academy Press), pp. 3–18.

INDEX

A Critica: Balbina, 56–57, 60–61
adaptive radiation, 26–7
AID (Agency for International
  Development), 114
Allen, R. N., 22, 42
alphabetizacao, 58
Altamira, x–xi, 63–4
  election of Prefeito, 76
  energy requirements, 66
  Kararao Dam effects, 68–71
  O Kaiapo, 81
Altamira–Xingu, 5, 63–72, &
  Fig. 5.1
Amancio, S. (FUNAI), 48–9
Amazon Alliance, 78–9, 109
Amazonia, 1–5 & Fig. 1.1
  boom–bust cycles, 6–9
  development, 6–15
  flooded areas, 36
Ambuklao Dam, Philippines, 22
Amnesty International, 98
Anchicaya Project, Columbian
  Amazon, 22
Anjudar, C. (CCPY), 80
assassinations, 79, 98
atmosphere and reservoirs, 24
Aukre (Indian village), 70

Babaquara Dam, 66–7
Balbina, ix, xi–xii
  2010 Plan, 96
  case study, 45–62 & Fig. 4.1 &
    Table 4.1
  flooding effects, 23–4, 36
  resistance, 57–62
  "scandal", 42, 60–61, 74
Barrow, C. Tucurui project, 23–4,
  24,28–9, 42, 45
Belem, xi, 68–9
Belem–Brasilia highway, 11
bioclimates, "life zones", 20–21

blindness, river: *Filaria*, 30
Blue Nile: schistosomiasis, 30
boom–bust cycles, 6–9
Boston Globe: World Bank refuses
  loan, 114–15
BR–174 highway, 48–51
Brasilia: new capital, 3, 10–11
brazil nut harvesters, 109–10
Brazilian Constitution: Indian
  guardianship, 31
Brazilian Socialist Party (Partido
  Socialista Braziliera: PSB), 59,
  76, 108
Brazilian Wilderness: T. Roosevelt,
  16
brazilwood, 6
Brokohondo Dam, Suriname, 24
Brundtland Commission Report,
  106
Bunker, S. G., Amazonian develop-
  ment, 7, 10–12
Burns, B. E., Amazonian develop-
  ment, 6, 8–13

Cabral, P., trader (1500), 6
Cachoieira Morena
  doubtful land ownership, 52
  riverine community, 51–2, 55–6
Cachoieira Porteira Hydroelectric,
  56–7, 69
Calha Norte 90, 92–3, Fig. 6.1
Carvajal, *Friar* G. de: explorer, 7,
  16
Catholic Indian Mission (CIMI),
  57–8, 82
Caufield, C., Brazil, energy and the
  Amazon, 22, 24, 26–7
CCPY (Committee for the Creation
  of the Yanomami Park), 80–81
CEDI (Ecumenical Centre
  for Documentation and

Information), xiv, 50, 87, 94, 114
Chagas disease (South American sleeping sickness), 29
Christianity: Indian conversions, 31
CIMI, *see* Indian Missionary Council
Clay, J., Cultural Survival, 109–10
coal resources, 103
colonial development, 3–7, 12–15, 78, 101
Columbian Amazon, Anchicaya Project, 22
Committee for the Creation of the Yanomami Park (Commisao para a Creacao do Parque Yanomami: CCPY), 80
concept manipulation, 100–101
"Conspiracy against Brazil", 97–8
Correa, S., journalist, 81
"counterfeit paradise", B. J. Meggers, 4, 16–17, 20, 30–31
CPI (Pro–Indian Commission), xiv, 82, 95–6
Cultural Survival, 109–10

Davis, S., *Victims of the Miracle*, 3,13, 49, 91
debts, national, 13, 107, 112
deculturalization, 3–4
deforestation, 3–4
deoxygenation effects, 23–4, 54
development
  Amazon River, 6–15
  poor and marginalized classes excluded, 102
  sustainable, 116
  university debates, 60
disease
  proliferation, 29–30
  vectors, 55

ecologists, 73–5, 108
  P. Fearnside, 20, 53, 61
economics
  foreign capital and debts, 10, 12–14, 42–3
  international lending institutions, 91–2
  national debts, 13, 107, 112

Ecumenical Centre for Documentation and Information (CEDI), 50, 94, 114
Eletrobras
  clashes with Indians, 95–6
  cost–benefit analysis, 72
  "depoliticization" of human issues, 99–101
  economic policy, 105–6
  government creation, 11
  plans, 34, 37–8, 40, 42
Eletronorte
  Altamira–Xingu complex, 64, 66–72
  Balbina, 45, 52–5, 57, 60–61
  incomplete studies, 42
  large projects, 105, 113
  opposition movements, 76–7, 85–6
  Public Relations Department, 74,
  use of chemical defoliants, 24,
endemicity, 27–8
energy
  alternatives, 102–7
  conservation, 104–5, 115
  production and consumption (1986–2010) 36–7 & Table 3.1
  transmission 40–41 & Fig. 3.3
Environmental Master Plan, 68
environmentalists, 59–62, 73–5, 108
eucalyptus plantations, 103
extinctions, species, 54, 55
extractive reserves, 108–109

Fearnside, P. ecologist, 20, 53, 61
Figueredo, G. P., 48–49
Filaria, river blindness, 30
firewood fuel, 103
fish and tree seeds, 23
floodplains, *varzea*, 11, 20
  communities and diversity, 23, 28
forests
  flooding and water cycles, 23–5
  Kayapo management, 28, 31–3
Frederico, *Padre*, 113
Friere, P., 58
fuel resources, 103–4
FUNAI, see National Indian Foundation

gas, natural, 103–4
Geisel Presidency, colonization
    projects, 12–13
glaciations, 27
gold strike: Yanomami, 92, 94
Goldsmith, E. and Hildyard, N.
    Social and environmental effects,
    22, 28–30, 53
Goodland, R. Evaluating tradeoffs,
    30, 42, 45
Goodyear, C. Rubber vulcanization,
    8
Goulart Presidency: nationali-
    sation, 11–12
Goverment control and "mega-
    products", 9–15
Grande Carajas Project, 33
"growth without development", E.
    Moran, 14–15

Havea brasiliensis, rubber trees, 8
Herrera, R. Nutrient cycling, 16, 21
highways
    Belem–Brazilia, 11
    BR–174, 48
    Transamazon, 12
    Transcontinental, 48
human rights activists/ native
    peoples, 79–88
hydro–development, 34–43, Fig. 3.1
    energy potential, 36
    indigenous peoples, 30–33
    large projects, 4–5
    small projects, 104–5 *see also*
        Balbina, Altamira–Xingu,
        Tucurui
*Hydroelectrics of the Xingu:
    The State Against the Indigenous
    People*, 82

IDESP,*see* Institute for Economic
    and Social Development of Para
IMF, *see* International Monetary
    Fund, 107
Imperatriz (FUNAI office), 83
Indian Missionary Council
    (Conselho Indigenista
    Missionario: CIMI), xiv, 57–8, 82,
    96–7, Fig. 6.1
    President's accident, 113–14
Indians

"civilization", 31–2
"Indian problem", 91–2
Indian rights bill, 87
O Kaiapo, 81
peasant antagonisms, 78–9, 108
population reductions, 7–8
resistance movements, 57–9, 72,
    79, 82–8
social exclusion, 76–7
see also FUNAI
"indicator species", 26
industry
    development, 9–10, 95
    energy consumption, 37–8
INPA (National Institute for
    Amazon Research), xiv, 55,
    61, 104–5
insect diversity, 25
Institute for Economic and Social
    Development of Para (Instituto
    do Desenvolvimento Economica e
    Social do Para: IDESP), 70
inter–regional electricity flux,
    38–9, Fig. 3.2
international lending institutions,
    91–2
International Monetary Fund
    (IMF), 107
International Rivers Network, 95
International Tropical Timber
    Organisation (ITTO), 109
Iriri river and dam, 66
Itumbiara hydroelectric, 56

Jurua (Indian village), 71

Kaiapo, P. P. (Chief), 33, 70, 83–7
Kamna (civilization), 49
Kararao, xi, 40, 64–72, Fig. 5.1
    Labour Unions, 52, 59, 76
    resistance, 73, 76, 82, 85, 110
Kayapo
    forest management, 28, 31–3
    ignorance of construction
        plans, 95
    resistance movements, 83–8
    unified resistance, 110
Kube–i (Chief), 83–5, 87
Kubitschek Presidency: Brasilia
    (1960), 10–11

Lake Michigan: decreased rainfall, 24
lakes, man made and disease, 29–30, 49
Landem, L. Non–governmental organizations, 111
Lange, A. Eletronorte social worker, 52, 77
leishmaniasis, 55
leito, night bus, 63
"life zones", bioclimates, 20–21

malaria, 29–30, 49, 55
Malaysia
    Penan arrests, 97
    Temengor Dam, 28
Manaus
    Balbina, 45–6, 48–51, 56, 58, 61
    opera house, 8
Medici Presidency: Waimiri-Atroari Reserve, 46
medicine: "folk", 28, 31–2
mega-projects, 6, 9–15
Meggers, B. J. "Counterfeit Paradise", 4, 16–17, 20, 30–31
Mendes, C., 78–9, 98, 108
Miami conference: rainforests 83–4
migrants, 63–4
    see also peasants
military rule
    (1964–1985), 12
    control of northern perimeter, 90, 92
minerals: exploitation, 50, 71
mining effects 92, 94 & Table 6.1
monkeys: "salvage", 54–5
Monosowski, E. Tucurui Dam environmental costs, 22, 33, 42
Moran, E. "Growth without development", 14–15
mosquitoes, *Anopheles*, 29–30, 49
Movement to Support the Waimiri-Atroari Resistance (MAREWA), xi–xii, xiv
    E. Schwade, 57–9, 77–8, 80
Myers, N. *The Primary Source*, 23, 26

National Indian Foundation (Fundacao Nacional dos Indios: FUNAI) x, xiv

legal representation, 79–80, 83, 87
"protective measures", 51, 70–71
S. Amancio, 48–9
National Indian Service (SPI), 91
National Institute for Amazon Research (Instituto Nacional para Pesquizes do Amazonia: INPA), xiv, 55, 61, 104–105
National Plan for Integration (PIN), xiv, 12–13, 78, 91
National Rubber Tappers Council, 109
national security (*segurarica nacional*), 90
Nationalists' policies, 9–10
native peoples/ human rights activists, 79–88
Nemec, J. Reesevervoirs and the atmosphere, 24
"New Republic", 89–90
New York Rainforest Alliance, viii
New York Times
    construction mistakes, 107
    press freedom, 74
Nigeria: soil loss and forest clearance, 21
non–governmental organizations (NGOS), xiv, 74
    resistance, 80, 85, 88, 110–11
nutrient cycling, 16, 21

O Estado de Sao Paulo
    Balbina scandal, 60–61
    "conspiracy against Brazil", 97–8
    electricity costs, 56–7
O Kaiapo: Indian newspaper, 81
O Liberal. Indian resistance, 83–4
onchocerciasis (river blindness), 29
"Operation Amazon" (1966), 12
overcrowding and sanitation, 30

Panama rainforests, viii
Paquicamba (Indian village), 71
Paranapanema mining firm, 50, 90
Partido des Trabalhadores (Workers' Party: PT), xiv, 59, 218
Partido Socialista Brasiliera (Socialist Party: PSB), xiv, 59, 108

PCP (sodium pentachlorrophenol):
defoliant, 24
peasants (farmers and migrants),
51–2, 77–9, 88
Penan tribals, 97
petroleum imports, 103, 105
Philippines, Ambuklao Dam, 22
PIN (National Plan for
Integration), xiv, 12–13, 78, 91
pistoleiros, 14
"Plano 2010", 34–43, Figs. 3.1–3.3,
Table 3.1, 95–96, 105
Pleistocene periods, 27
Polamazonia project (1974), 13
politics
development, 89–101, Fig. 6.1,
Table 6.1
minority parties, 76–9
Posey, D. A.
Kayapo forest management,
28, 31–3
Kayapo resistance, 83–5, 87, 113
Presidencies, *see* Figueredo, Geisel,
Goulart, Kubitschek and Medici
Presidente Figueredo, xi–xii, 48–9,
55, 57–9
press freedom, 74
Primary Source, The, N. Myers, 1,
19–20, 23, 26–7
Pro–Indian Commission (CPI), xiv,
82, 95–6
proalcool (sugar cane), 103
PSB (Brazilian Socialist Party), xiv,
76, 108
PT (Workers' Party), xiv, 76–7,
108

rainfall
Lake Michigan, 24
tropical rainforests, 19
Rainforest Action Network, xiii, 97
rainforests, dams, 16–32
refugia, 27–8
reservoirs and the atmosphere, 24
Resistance
Balbina, 57–62
fragmentation, 107–108
strengthening, 107–112
Xingu complex, 72–88
Rondonia: mining, 94, Table
6.1

Roosevelt, T., *Brazilian Wilderness*,
16
Roraima: mining, 92, Table 6.1
Rosa, L. P. and Schaffer, R., fuel
resources, 103–114
rubber
Asian plantations, 8
boom, 8
Tappers of Acre, 78–9, 98, 108–9
Rural Agricultural Workers' Union
(*Syndicato*), 52, 59, 76

Samuel Dam, 36
sanitation and overcrowding, 30
Sao Francisco river, 56
Sao Paulo
energy transmission, 4, 40–41,
Fig. 3.3
founding of permanent colonies
(1532), 7
Kararao: importation of
electricity, 66–7
newspapers, 74
Sarawak: Penan tribals, 97
schistosomiasis, 30
Schwade, E. (MAREWA), xii, 46,
49–50, 57–8, 78–80
Schwartzman, S., and Allegretti, M.
H., extractive reserves, 109
sedimentation effects, 22
segurarica nacional (national
security), 90
SEMA (Special Secretary for the
Environment), 60
siltation: M. A. Allen, 22, 42
slave labour and trade, 7, 46
sleeping sickness, Chagas disease,
29
sloths
salvage, 54
specialized relationships, 26
snail vectors, schistosomiasis, 30
social justice/ minority political
parties, 76–9
Society for the Preservation of
Natural Resources and Cultures
of Amazonia (Sociadade para
a Preservacao dos Recoursos
Naturais e Culturais da
Amazonia: SOPREN), xiv, 74–5
soils

bioclimates, 20–21
erosion, 21–2
nutrient cycling, 21
poor quality, 16, 20, 52
tropical and dams, 20–22
SOPREN, *see* Society for the Preservation of Natural Resources and Cultures of Amazonia
Special Secretary for the Environment (SEMA), 60
species
diversity, 25–6
losses to reservoirs, 25–9
SPI (National Indian Service), 91
sugar
boom, 7
cane (proalcool), 103
surveillance, government, 113
Survival International, 109
"Syndicato" (Rural Agricultural Workers' Union), 52, 59, 76

Tapupuna relocation, 51
Taquari relocation, 51,
Temengor Dam, Malaysia, 28
Tennessee Valley Authority, 29
terra firma: inland forest, 20, 27
Tocantins river, 28–9
Tosi, J. A. "life zones", bioclimates, 20–21
tradeoffs evaluation: R. Goodland, 29–30, 42
Transamazon highway, 12, 49, 63–4, 68, 70
Transcontinental Highway, 48
transmission of energy 40–41, Fig. 3.3
tree seeds and fish, 23
TRFs, *see* tropical rainforests
tribal groups: reductions, 3
Trincheiro (Indian village), 71
Tropical Forestry Action Plan, 106
tropical rainforests (TRFs)
definition 17–20, Fig. 2.1
diversity of ecosystems, 25–7
endangered species, 28
primary and secondary, 19–20
soils, 20–22
Tucurui, 4, 42, 45, 96
disease proliferation, 29

flooding effects, 23–4, 33, 36, 50
incomplete studies, 42
soil erosion, 22
species lost, 28–9
summary of problems, 75
2010 Plan, *see* "Plano 2010"

Uatama River, 45
underdevelopment of the Amazon, 14–15
UNEP (United Nations Environmental Programme), 79, 83
UNI (Union of Indigenous Nations), 82–3, 87
Union of Indigenous Nations (UNI), 82–3, 87,109
United Nations Environmental Programme (UNEP), 79, 83
United States
funding, 43, 114, 115
treatment of Brazil, 112

varzea, floodplains, 11, 20
communities and diversity, 23, 28, 56
Viana, C., (SOPREN), 74–5
Vitoria: threatened town, 68–9
Viveros de Castro, E. and Andrade L. M. M., 95, 99–101
Volta River, Africa, 30

Waimiri–Atroari, xi–xii
history, 80
MAREWA, 57–9
mining projects, 92, 94
population decline, 45–6, Tab. 4.1
reserve, 48–52, Fig. 4.1
Washington Post, 109
water cycles and forest flooding, 23–5
Wickham, A. Smuggled rubber seeds (1876), 8
"Wild West": Presidente Figueredo, xii
"wildlife salvage" programmes, 54–5
Workers' Party (Partido dos Trabalhadores: PT), 59, 76–7, 108
World Bank

energy development programme,
    66, 68
extractive reserves, 109
limited public information, 96
non compliance with loan
    conditions 84
rejection of Power sector loan, 84,
    114–15 App.
review loan requests, 13
World Wildlife Fund research
    site, xi

Xingu
    Hydroelectric Complex, 64–72
    resistance, 72–88

Yanomami
    Committee for the Creation
        of the Yanomami Park
        (CCPY), 80–81
    Indian territory, 80–81, 83
Yanomami, D.: UNEP award, 83

Zuazo, R., viii–ix, xii, 113–14

For Product Safety Concerns and Information please contact our EU
representative GPSR@taylorandfrancis.com Taylor & Francis Verlag GmbH,
Kaufingerstraße 24, 80331 München, Germany

Printed and bound by CPI Group (UK) Ltd, Croydon, CR0 4YY
01/05/2025
01858357-0004